REvision

2000 YEAR OLD PRINCIPLES THAT ARE RELEVANT FOR WOMEN ENTREPRENEURS TODAY

Reverend Claudia W. Spradley

REvision: 2000 Year Old Principles that are Relevant for Women Entrepreneurs Today

©2017 Claudia W. Spradley

All rights reserved. No portion of this book may be reproduced, stored in retrieval system, or transmitted in any form or by any means- electronic, mechanical, photocopy, recording, scanning, or other – except for brief quotation in critical reviews or articles, without the prior written permission of the publisher.

Unless otherwise noted, scripture quotations are taken from The Maxwell Leadership Bible, New King James Version (NKJV) Bible ©2007 by Thomas Nelson, Inc. Quotations from this source are not a substantial contribution to the content of this book.

Published in West Palm Beach, Florida, by The Spradley Dunn Group.

REvision may be purchased in bulk for educational, business, fund-raising, or sales promotional use. For information please email spraddunn@yahoo.com

ISBN 978-0-9990418-0-2

Library of Congress Cataloging-In-Publication Data

Cover and interior design by Stacey Grainger

DEDICATION

REvision is dedicated to my daughters, Linda, Stephanie, Avis, and Keisha, who were raised to be career minded professional women. And, to my granddaughters Aarolyn, Alysse, Anna, Amanda, Andeidre, and Alexandra.

TABLE OF CONTENTS

	Acknowledgements	vi
Chapter 1	Eve: The Truth Teller	7
Chapter 2	Jezebel: The Queen	23
Chapter 3	Mary: The Magdalene	39
Chapter 4	Priestess of Endor: The Sibyl	57
Chapter 5	Deborah: The General Judge	77
Chapter 6	Thecla: The Preacher	93
Chapter 7	Rahab: The Business Woman Renown	113
Chapter 8	Lydia: The Ultimate Business Woman	131
Chapter 9	Woman: The Virtuous One	147
Chapter 10	Women of Today: Take Action	161
Appendix A	Personal Mission Statement	163
Appendix B	Personal Vision Statement	164
Appendix C	Definition of Self Statement	165
Appendix D	Personal Self-Care Plan	166
Appendix E	The Life Ledger	168
	References	170
	About the Author	173

ACKNOWLEDGMENTS

Many thanks to my Linda. While my head was in the clouds communing with spirits, making up stories and such, Linda's business sense kept us firmly tethered to the ground throughout this collaboration. I cherish the days of working together to make this a finished product. Mothers and daughters get along just fine, though fierce. Love you!

Stephanie and Kira…thanks for taking care of the logistics of the "thing" and managing the details of travel with care. You are the best ever!

Avis, you are the best morale and 'meds' keeper. Thanks for your ever cheerful smile and acting as "listening post" for some of the strange ideas we discussed. Luv ya'…girl.

Keisha, your phone calls ending with "Luv you Mumsie" kept me lifted for days. Love you back. You too, Karress.

Rufus Jr., and Michelle… we travelled well together. Thanks for always getting me 'here and there', and always on time…even through the hurricane…remember?

Rufus Sr., thank you for all you did! You know what…you know when. Thanks much!

Adam, Chris, and Shaina…your music soothed my spiritual soul! And Charles Jr., you kept my physical soul fed with that great cooking.

My everlasting thanks and love to Van Dunn, Moses Brown, and Isaac Holland. I still miss you Charles Sears.

Thanks to my friend, the Reverend E. Gene Dixon, mentor and comrade in arms on the battlefield! Our many theological discussions served to sharpen my research skills and diminish my "irreverence." My hands are still on the gospel plow, thanks to you!

Thanks also to Aarolyn, Alysse, Andeidre, Amanda, and Anna for reading and listening to my "stuff" and laughing at the right places. Your youthful points of view offered much perspective and humor. Love you dearly. You are the best granddaughters any one could ask for. Yes Alexandra, you too!!

Aaron (A.J.), thanks for hanging out with me! My Sunday cooking was mainly for you.

Dedra N. Tate, thanks much. You did a fantastic job.

Dr. Larthenia Howard…THANK YOU for seeing my vision.

I am so grateful that the family saga continues in Deborah, Charlee, Alana, Nyala, Ariel, Camryn, and Charles III. God bless us, everyone.

AUTHOR'S PREFACE

REvision is a collection of stories as experienced by outstanding women in The Bible, but told from different perspectives than you have likely ever heard. Although the characters are the same and the stories remain unchanged, the way in which they viewed significant events were different. The familiar saying, "there are three sides to every story," is indeed a possible truth. This is especially enlightening considering The Bible as we know it was primarily written by men, with little articulation from women. Women were not highly regarded at the time and had a limited voice to express events from their perspectives. Many historical female figures have had to record events under a pseudonym, oftentimes as a man. This was not different for biblical events. Many were not even identified by name, or their stories were completely erased. However, by studying, we know women have influenced the development of what we now recognize as Christianity, and also other religions. Women, though deemed lower than men and treated as secondary citizens, were among the most notable movers and shakers of their time. They made their own money, ran businesses as CEO, COO, and CFO, raised families, fought wars, and still found time to worship and serve the Living God.

By definition, revision suggests an update or new version, an adaptation or modification that spins the original into something different. This, however, is slightly different. *REvision* takes another look at the old and filters it through contemporary lens. This allows for new and alternative perspectives.

Perspective makes all the difference. Matthew 6:22-23 reads: *"The lamp of the body is the eye. If therefore your eye is good, your whole body will be full of light. But if your eye is bad, your whole body will be full of darkness. If therefore the light that is in you is darkness, how great is that darkness!"* Your frame of reference, the eye, as reflected in Scripture, serves to provide a framework for which observations can be judged. In other words, the events you perceive and the thoughts you act upon throughout your daily life are generally aligned with your beliefs. If you have a belief that things just don't work out for you, then you will find ways (though oftentimes unconsciously) to validate this belief. The opposite is also true. If you believe things almost always work out for you, you will look for evidence to confirm this to be the case. Either way, your perspective, or perception, determines how you internalize information that later produces behaviors. There is no doubt personal experiences, values, and beliefs foreshadow the way we experience life. Behaviors, actions, and reactions impact our views of the world and how we interact with those around us. Simply put, interpretations matter.

It has been said, *"How you see what you see, determines what you see."* Imagine looking at a beautiful piece of art through a kaleidoscope. What would you see? In all likelihood, fragments of color floating whimsically before you. Similar to a kaleidoscope, perspective offers opportunities to view things that seem static in completely new ways. This new observation changes reality, and consequently your belief systems. What once appeared one dimensional suddenly becomes multifaceted. The ability to alter how we see things can be empowering. When we learn to objectively view situations and to consider a multiplicity of choices, possibilities are increased.

REvision showcases influential women from the Bible and the messages, or lessons they have left for our inspiration. These lessons viewed through a contemporary lens will perhaps allow you to see and respond differently to the world. Whether you are a wife, mother, entrepreneur, homemaker, in middle management, or at the top of your game, the ability to see from multiple viewpoints is incumbent to your success.

As you engage in these recounts of life stories, *REvision* offers the curious mind an opportunity to reposition one's own life and engage in self-reflection. At the conclusion of each woman's narrative, lessons are extracted for consideration. The women you will encounter within these pages know about defeat, fear, triumph, business management, juggling responsibilities, unwavering commitment, the principles of creation and their responsibilities to the earth, and many other principles for living powerfully. The interactive exercises invite you to engage and discern practical applications. There is no doubt each of these women understood who they were and the values they shepherded in every circumstance they encountered.

Unapologetically, there are no questions of self-worth or birthrights. For, *"So, God created man in His own image; in the image of God He created him; male and female He created them. Then God blessed them,..."* (Genesis 1:27-28).

With an open mind and a spirit willing to challenge the difficulties in your daily walk, I encourage you to take a journey through history with these women in the Bible. You will witness heralding courage, the will to never give up, and an outreach of faith. If you listen, purposely listen, you will no doubt collect jewels that will positively accentuate even the most savvy contemporary lifestyle.

Blessings,

Reverend Claudia W. Spradley
Author, *REvision*

INTRODUCTION

Questions! Questions! Questions!
The "Irreverent" Reverend Claudia Speaks...

As a young girl in the church, and later as a young matron, I often listened to the preacher stomp, snort, and whoop his way through the Sunday sermon - extolling on the sins and evil misdoings of the shrewd, cunning, and powerful woman (Eve), and the helpless, hapless male, and his inability to withstand temptation (Adam). Questions crowded my mind.

What were they thinking?

Didn't they know a good thing when they saw it? All they had to do was eat, sleep, play, and take dominion of the Earth.

But then, another thought intruded.

The tree of life was set in the Garden of Eden, but it was not to be touched. So, if that tree was so dangerous, why did God put it there in the first place?

Are we dealing with a playful, fickle God?

Is this woman really to blame for an alleged fall?

What fall?

Was there really a fall? Another question.

If this woman who came as a helper had the power, the intelligence, and the manipulative ability to turn the world on a spin, shouldn't we preach about some of her good qualities?

After all, she was more God-like. She possessed within her the power and secrets of creation, the creation of life.

Couldn't we address her articulateness? Adam could only whine and grunt.

Couldn't we speak about her wanting wisdom, her ability to take charge, changing a child-like mentality to one of knowledge and decision making?

Was there a place to address her womanly essence, and of all things, that great fountain of power she possessed?

Even more, where could I get some of this power? I was thrown out of Bible class for that!

More questions popped up in my head despite my punishment, and because of a very curious and inquisitive mind, I delighted in asking questions for the sake of discussion. Sometimes I received answers that were either mumbled, obscure, made no sense, or so farfetched, even the most dimwitted would find humor. One of my fondest discussions went much like this:

"Where did Cain get his wife?"

"God prepared him a wife!"

"How? Did he pluck her from a tree, pull her out of thin air? Snatch her out of the sea?" Or, "Did he take one of his sisters?"

Gasps!

"If they were the first and only people, then who lived there, or was there an infamous land of Nod? Was the Garden of Eden merely an experimental laboratory designed to record the evolutionary progress of a species?"

Gasps and swoons!

"Was Cain's exile really punishment, or profound relief as he exited a restricted and harsh living situation of serving an egotistical, stern and angry God?"

After all, he got to travel, walked around with his woman, met other people, hunted and gathered food. He even started a new society and served a more benevolent, friendlier God. Ideal living!

Later, sitting through meetings and endless sermons, we listened to exhorters and teachers as they expounded on the virtues of a woman's submissiveness (Ephesians 6) to her husband. From the innermost recesses of my brain - to my mouth - to all the air and ears around me came a very loud, WHY? Why would a supposed loving, and very wise God require the completed perfection of creation to be in submission to the un-perfected part? Wasn't the first Adam really just a rough draft?

The preacher held the Word (KJV) aloft and responded in a rasping, stentorian voice designed to send demons back to the spawning grounds: "It's in this Book, written for all to see and read!"

I responded calmly and with no meanness of heart, "Then, that particular part of the book must be wrong."

Gasps, swoons, and vapors.

After long minutes of complete stillness and utter shock, I was prayed on, prayed to, and prayed for. I was also thrown out of the meeting, again! Still questioning.

Even so, there was something within me, urging me to keep asking questions and looking for answers. Something stirred within me, and I knew there was more to be understood. I was urged to keep asking and searching. Something said, "In every society, every culture, there are those who question, or seek answers. The answers will come."

In response to a compelling power, coaxing me to preach and to teach, I entered the doors of the seminary and found discussions encouraged, and questions debated. The studies of Greek, Latin, and Hebrew were as soothing balms to my questing mind. I learned the true meaning of the word "exegesis." Translations and other books excited me. I was now ready to explore the "woman's issues" in the Bible and in history. Then came the explosion of Feminist and Womanist Theology and "herstories." Eagerly, I joined the fray.

I began to research the lives of ancient women, pagan women, biblical women, mythical women, and divine women. In the process, I wrote a drama entitled, "Great Women of the Bible: Telling Their True Stories." I recruited some very brave and talented women in the churches and traveled the state, performing in churches and halls for Women's Day, Mother's Day, Fifth Sunday, Missionary Day, and any other day we were invited. We encountered anger, joy, surprise, and affirmations of the Word. Some of the elder sisters and mothers would bless us with a sigh and a heartfelt Amen, as if saying, "here is the real story at last."

The drama began with ten characters. At the end of each performance, I would hear the women's spirits in my heart and in my mind. Sounds of, "Tell my story. Tell my story. It's time for the truth." Many times during a performance, the anointing of the Holy Spirit would fall, and the women would become one with their character. Phoebe would preach. Mary Magdalene would shed tears and proclaim in song as the first witness of the resurrected Lord. Miriam would dance for joy with a tambourine. At other times, the spirits of women, not on the program would make their appearance. As narrator or redactor, I would improvise the script to accommodate these demanding and assertive spirits. The elders would call out, "Quench not the Spirit and let the women come forth!"

As I continued in study, preaching, teaching, giving performances, conducting workshops and seminars on church history, the Bible, and women's issues, brethren became angry, agitated, and sometimes confrontational. Some muttered, some shouted, and others just sat and glowered at me. And still, others would applaud my efforts to enlighten and bring knowledge. Often, women in their very tight chains would say to me, "Stop making trouble for us in the church." They would counsel me to be more humble and docile, less outspoken. But I could not. The spirits of those forgotten women were upon me. I soon realized that a compulsion, a geas, had been placed upon me. I had to continue to speak out and write about these women who had done so much in history, those who had their lives maligned, spirits quenched, and were hidden. Many of their lives, messages, and stories had been twisted, redacted, obliterated, or lost in the scriptures. I retrieved them.

With an opened mind, I started the journey of discovering the spirits of women. I walked in the places they walked - the streets, paths, and trails. I touched the stones they touched, and allowed nothing to deter me from speaking the truth about their lives. I was not given a spirit of fear, but one of truth and discernment. And, so my holy treks began. What a journey it has been! Each woman, with her own distinct personality, has come through the pages of her story with courage and a sense of justice, vindication, and righteousness fulfilled.

Chapter 1
EVE: THE TRUTH TELLER

In the Beginning

The first woman who spoke to me and started me on the quest was Eve, and rightly so. Off to Africa I flew. Her spirit persisted and labored far into the night with me. I was not allowed to rest until this chapter was written. Eve was not the docile, empty-headed child who was easily tempted by a serpent. Her spirit was presented as an assertive, decision making, take charge sister with a made-up mind. Is the creation a myth, a story, or the truth?

Sister Eve Speaks…

Fall?

What fall?

My story. My life has been so twisted, so analyzed, dissected, lied about, and redacted, until I was sometimes unsure of the events that transpired in the alleged "Garden of Eden." Many have written about me, but this is the first time I am able to speak my own words and tell my own story. Some say I was nothing more than a myth, a legend, a story to explain the beginnings of the human race. Well, all nations of people have created national epics and sagas to establish their origin as a people upon the earth -to give credibility to their divineness and Deities. And, they all have common themes of healing waters, magic blood or ichor, mystical holy symbols, arks, swords, horns, grails, hammers, or such. They portray wise people, oracles (usually women), heaven and hell, divine messengers, spirits, angels, or doves. Beatrice, Mercury, Apollo, the Valkyries, Gabriel, and most of all, a hero or heroine chosen to be manipulated by an intervening, or interfering, god or goddess. Moses, Paris, Roland, Jesus, Mary, Beowulf, and the Oshun, were given special powers to right some wrongs, or otherwise to sacrifice themselves for the greater good. Oh yes, there was always a battle to be fought, and lots of trickery and deceit. And magical animals, serpents, flying horses, nurturing wolves, talking birds, and dragons – always requiring blood sacrifices.

Anyway, back to the garden.

I was created as one who came to the aid of the man, to help him to run this world. He was definitely in over his head. He was a rough draft. I was the perfection of creation. Genesis 3 states that we are the "imago dei," made in the image of God and goddess. I was created with the desire for knowledge, wisdom, and decision-making power. I had lots of other kinds of powers, secret woman powers given to me by the goddess. The Shekinah. The power of creation, nurturing and life bringing, was deep within me.

When I got here, the place was a mess! Chickens were flapping about, dogs were running everywhere, birds flying and swooping, the lions trying to eat the lambs. There were bears and ants in the honeycombs, pigs polluting the water, and fruits and vegetables not harvested. I immediately got busy, setting things right and making things pretty - laying patterns, picking and planting flowers, testing herbs and plants for food. And him, lying under the trees asleep! Hmmmm…no shelter. Where were we supposed to sleep? In the trees I guess. We could always catch the links of vines and swing down in the mornings. When the man awoke, he called me something, but my name is Eve, bringer of life. He couldn't do a thing but whine and grunt.

Goddess, spare me this!

But, I went on about my business of setting up seasonal days, solstices, equinoxes, and such. That was hard work. I had to keep track of the seasonal changes in the weather, the stars, and voices of nature. I had to tell him when to come in out of the rain and mist!

After several changing of the seasons, and waxings and wanings of the moon, I got the feeling that I was being watched. Uh! Uh! This should prove interesting. I was getting bored because that man was off somewhere playing "war" with his God, and I was dying for some decent conversation. I hoped it would be somebody or even something with a vocabulary of more than five words.

One day, I turned the corner by the big tree, and there he, or it, was. A man. A snake. Something good to look at and something to talk to. I could see the light of intelligence in its eyes.

Okay. This might work.

I invited him to come over and eat with me and stop all that peeping and spying! I served him some of that delicious fruit I found in the far east corner near the lake.

He asked me if I knew that this fruit would make me more God-like and wise!

I laughed! I'm already God-like and wise. I was created that way. I've been eating this fruit since I came here. Maybe I should give some to the man, Adam.

Lord knows he needed all the help he could get. The man's brain was like a bowl of Jell-O, clear, bland, and shaky.

Well, I did! I gave him a dish of nice, chilled, sliced fruit and he ate it with a big smile because it tasted so delicious. Then, all of a sudden, he jumped up all crazy-like and started screaming at me and yelling something about God having told us not to eat this fruit or we would surely die!

I yelled back, "If He told you that, why did you eat it? He didn't tell me that nor did you tell me that. I've been eating this fruit since I got here and I'm not dead! Sit down and calm yourself. We can work this out. Stop whimpering…You're not going to die!"

We sat and I tried to talk some sense into him. But no way, he just kept crying and carrying on, and muttering something about disobedience!

My friend wasn't much help…just sitting there laughing at that poor scared man. I was getting very concerned for him.

Well, when God came walking through that evening, calling for him (I was never included in these little tete-a-tete of theirs), Adam jumped up to run to Him, but I stopped him!

"Wait a minute," I said. "Fix yourself up, comb your hair, wash your face and put on this cute little leaf apron I made for you. Look nice for your company. Now just go out there and explain things. Let Him know that I was not told of His desire to keep that tree for Himself - landlord vs. tenants' rights thing. Hold your head up. Stop looking at the ground! Now go on.!"

But things did not go well.

First, He was angry because we put on some clothes. Then, Adam went out there and started whining about my forcing him to eat this fruit.

Forcing him!

Well, I decided to go out there and defend myself, and I also wanted answers to a couple of heated questions.

First, I wanted to know why did He put that tree there if it would cause so much damage? And second, were we supposed to be like little children, naked, brainless playthings, running around without a thought in our heads, and just to keep Him company when He felt like playing?

Obedience with no understanding or wisdom? I didn't think so!

Well, He did not like my being so brash as to question Him!

He started talking about curses…mean stuff.

He told Adam, who was shaking, trembling and falling all over the ground, that he had to work for a living.

Huh!

No pity from me. I was already working. Who do you think was keeping that garden in good order?

He turned to the pretty thing that had talked and visited with me, and before my very eyes that thing slithered to the ground and turned into an ugly old snake. Then, it had the nerve to try and bite my foot. I proceeded to stomp the heck out of it. Busted his head up quite nicely. Bite me will you? Not this sister! Wisdom told me to take care of myself, and I did. That is one snake that will never walk again. Not with a broken back, crushed head and ribs, and a ripped off tail.

Now the great Himself turned those angry eyes my way. He never liked me that much, and said I loved Wisdom, Sophia, too much.

Then, He proceeded to pronounce curses on me. He said that I would bear babies in pain and labor.

And why is that a curse? Because He couldn't have babies! Anyway, what babies? I'm pregnant? And from whom? Adam or that serpent? I spent a lot of time with both of them.

He also said something about me loving only my husband. I guess that's chastisement for being good friends with the serpent, or whatever the heck it was. Besides, who else was there in that place, since he just turned my "friend" into a snake.

Well, anyway, we were evicted from our home in the Garden - without even a thirty days' notice, and had to move down into the valley to start over. That was okay. Eden was very confining, but the valley was pretty.

But in the hurried move, I left some of my things - leaf skirts, clay pots, special dried herbs and such, and I wanted some more of that fruit.

I was craving like crazy.

So back up the hill and through the vale I went.

When I got to the gate, I was shocked! There standing at the entrance were two angels with burning swords barring my way. I would have taken the angels on, but those swords were another matter. Flames shooting out everywhere!

Uh! Uh! Some landlords are so petty.

But never fear. I had a plan. Thanks to Wisdom, sisters always have plans 1, 2, and maybe 3. I'd wait 'til dark, go around back, slip through the hedges and get some of the windblown seeds, fallen fruit, and a few cuttings to plant my own trees. The valley was quite fertile. They would grow well there. Plus, I had to find that special herb. If I was going to live for over 150 years, I needed to take control of this fertility thing. I would decide when I wanted to have some more children. I didn't want to spend all of my time taking care of babies and watering plants. I planned to do some traveling…see the rest of the world…study the skies…. chart the seasons…spend more time with Wisdom, gaining more knowledge, and definitely more power. First mother, first wife. First grandmother and full of womanly power. Lilith had the good sense not to marry. She just left with no ties.

There was something else that was good about that fruit too, it worked on Adam. He learned to communicate…somewhat!

What Eve Knows

Set an Intention

In all of her candor and feistiness, there is no doubt Eve was on a mission. She had the world to conquer and an attitude to make it happen. Although she seemed to wander around the garden at times, she did so with insight and a sense of meaning. She knew what she was looking for and set on a path to find what she wanted. The revelation of her mission showed great confidence - a commission to help man. With clarity and purpose, Eve had a relentless proclivity to take initiative and to take audacious action. By all means, she was determined to carry out her mission in life.

While it is common for businesses and organizations to build focus and direction through mission statements, individuals rarely define such a statement of personal power. A clearly defined mission statement portrays the perception of permanence and outlines relevancy. Intentions connect expectations and resources that float in and around the universe. Targeted, there is creation that is both compelling and impactful. In itself, intention commands energy. This is the seed that accomplishes dreams and spurs the pursuit of your desires.

Just as in an organization, a well written personal mission statement brands the individual with purpose and guidance. Daily activity can be more clearly measured and tracked based on direction by the mission. Behaviors become meaningful, purposeful, and directed, rather than haphazard. A set intention, or mission, establishes a foundational navigation through which fulfillment in life flows.

---

*"Outstanding people have one thing in common:
An absolute sense of mission."*

Zig Ziglar
American Author, Motivational Speaker

Create a *Personal Mission Statement*. If you have a written statement, review it and be sure the intended focus is where your efforts are directed.

See an example of a personal statement in Appendix A.

What measures or tracking system will you use to monitor alignment of your Personal Mission and actual outcomes?

Inspect the Expected

From her perspective, Eve was not involved in the messaging of God's expectations to avoid eating from the forbidden tree. By her account, she was not asked, told, or given clear guidance about what to eat or not to touch in the garden. Because expectations were not clearly defined, or inspected, she acted upon the little information received and devised her own perceptions. Like in so many failed interactions, perceptions can be deceiving and misguiding. In successful communication, it is necessary to survey others in order to gather data that leads to outcomes or services that both meet and exceed expectations.

To inspect the expected is to suggest a close examination or probing of the desired outcomes. In the process, you will call upon retrospection to inform an intentional course of action. What worked and what didn't work in the past? Armed with this information, introspection can be crystallized and communicated with clarity.

When you interact with family, friends, prospects, clients, or teams within your organization, it is imperative to understand the expectations of each person involved and to also communicate expectations from your viewpoint. Building relationships on "perceived" needs can prove costly. An extra effort to ask questions and study the needs of others, or the market if you are in business, is exercising plain ole' good sense. It is senseless to build relationships or offer a product or service that does not meet the expectations of the intended audience. Likewise, disappointment and resentment ensue when your expectations are not reciprocated. By establishing expectations at the onset of interactions, you help minimize discrepancies in final outcomes.

What systems do you have in place to receive feedback from others related to expectations? How do you clearly communicate your expectations?

Maintaining relevance is essential in sustaining growth. What is your plan to ensure relevance and progressiveness?

Communicate, Communicate, and Communicate

There must have been a misunderstanding of sorts, between God's instruction of the forbidden tree and Eve's ability to rationalize defiance of the command. It became apparent soon after her creation that Eve would play a huge role in the wellbeing of man. Her ability to corral others (Adam) to take part in her endeavors, whether good or bad, was evidence that communication is an art form. A form of art that requires skill, eloquence, and poise.

Within any interaction, effective communication is among one of the most significant tools. When open paths of communication are not accessible at all levels, both negative and incorrect information are viable. The promotion of candid and meaningful information-sharing cultivates the likelihood of cohesiveness and positive impact. The seemingly blurred lines of communication between Adam and Eve demonstrate the gravity of failed effectiveness. In doing so, details are ignored, and accountability is scarce.

A consciousness of communication patterns is necessary to create an environment where feedback and the sharing of ideas, especially those that appear to be in contrast to the norm, are accepted, appreciated, and valued. Communication has often been deemed the great influencer. The more effectively you communicate, the more influence you spread. When you develop and share ideas in a way that steers others toward and buy-in to your vision, you create influence. Positively or negatively, communication influences involvement and outcomes.

"The single biggest problem in communication is the illusion that it has taken place."

George Bernard Shaw
Playwright, Critic, and Polemicist

Recall a time when your communication was misinterpreted or misrepresented. Given your experience, how would you have communicated differently?

Identify your patterns of communication. How do you generally respond when in disagreement with an idea or thought that really matters? Is there anything you would consider changing in your usual pattern of communication?

Chapter 2
JEZEBEL: THE QUEEN

Insanity and Survival of the Fittest

Often, when studying a particular scriptural text or paragraph with deep intensity, one sentence or one word will carry thoughts down rabbit trails to entirely new trains of thinking, causing one to emit that very satisfying "aha!" Such was the case when I was deeply engrossed in the exegesis of scriptures concerning the Queen, Jezebel, whose very name invokes images of moral looseness, promiscuity, and retribution. Why was this woman so slandered? So hated? I saw these verses of scripture as yet another chapter in the eternal struggle between Yahweh and the female deity Ashtoreth, or goddess Shekinah.

Baal was a collection of lesser gods in service to her! Long before Jezebel came to rule the land, Baal worship was a fact in Israel. The Yahweh cult gained prominence through fighting, brutality, and borrowing the rituals and beliefs from Baal, who was then made into Yahweh's enemy. Most of the warring and fighting was to establish Yahweh as the one true God and to diminish the power and influence of the pagan gods. Even so, the Baal cult remained strong because it was primarily associated with women and the supreme goddess Ashtoreth. The high-ranking queens, Jezebel, and royalty from other lands, were priestesses of the cults, ordained to perform rituals and rites of the orders. As I read passages from the book of Jeremiah, it became exceedingly clear; women were neither passive nor docile in their worship, but rather they were emphatic and assertive in their beliefs and rituals. When Jeremiah threatened them with destruction and damnation in chapter 17, railing and weeping, saying they were making cakes for the feast days of the Queen of Heaven, pouring out libations, and drinking wine, they answered with a great defiance and determination:

"But we will certainly do whatever has gone out of our own mouth, to burn incense to the queen of heaven and pour out drink offerings to her, as we have done, we and our fathers, our kings and our princes, in the cities of Judah and in the streets of Jerusalem...."

Jerimiah 44:17

In the old prophets' railings and condemnations, women were always blamed for leading the people astray. According to Christopher Whitcombe, in his article, "Eve and the Identity of Women," although the idea the prophets wished to convey was one of relapse from Yahwism, it was not difficult to discern that the Baal cult was well established and widespread in the ancient world. Much of the Old Testament can be seen as a propaganda tract against Baal. The tactic adopted by the Yahwists in their efforts to defeat Baal was to demonize the cult and represent Baal as an evil god, hostile to humankind, while portraying Yahweh as a kind, benevolent, and loving God, forced to be harsh and murderous when his children strayed.

Why would a god be forced into anything? Forced into warfare and murder? Was this the writers' way of justifying the fighting and greed of a war-faring, land stealing, people? Creating a God with human qualities and a carnal nature? A God fashioned like themselves?

Will these struggles never end? Will there ever be a time of peace on earth? Will the goddess Gaia grow weary of the fighting and destruction loosed upon this earth and simply shrug and cause the world to cease to exist? Will men ever win over their brutal warlike nature and their need to dominate everybody and everything? Or, throw deadly toys and temper tantrums when they can't? Will spirituality and love ever return to religion, or has there ever been? Will we stop fighting in the name of false gods and man-made rules? Man-made gods? And false rules?

What manner of glory is to be found in muddy, bloodied battlefields filled with dying groans and agonized cries? What kind of love is shown by dying for a piece of cloth with painted symbols? Is manhood measured by the amount of pain one can withstand, or facing death with stoicism and tightly suppressed agony? Isn't life more precious than a jeweled ornament? How much land does a person need? How much love does a human need? What is gained by giving one's life for a plot or piece of ground? The irony of it all…to die and then be buried in the same ground you died for.

As I traveled from the Phoenician coast to the heart of the biblical land of the ancients, I was stunned by the quietness and stark beauty of this land that had been so scarred by war and pestilence. I viewed Mt. Carmel, where the infamous challenge between Yahweh and the Queen of Heaven took place. We traveled through dry deserts with the wind whipping our scarves from our faces, revealing our dried eyes and wind-chapped lips. Sunglasses and oily chapstick were as essential as bottled water and tissue.

Jezebel, the Queen, Speaks…

Arrogant? Yes! Conceited? Yes! Rich? Educated? Refined? Aggressive? A born ruler? Yes! Yes! Yes!

But I was not a loose, promiscuous woman!

I was a queen and a priestess, devoted to my goddess and her worship. I was devoted because of love. Elijah was devoted to his

God because of fear! I was born a Phoenician princess, sitting high in the royal court of my father, King Ethbaal. I was taught the ins and outs of ruler-ship early, and I was steeped in royalty.

When Omri, king of some little nation on the African coast, wanted to secure his treaty with my father, he offered his son Ahab to me in marriage. I did not want this, but he pointed out the political advantages this would have for both nations. No love… just politics and economics. Children of royalty are raised as pawns in political games, taught to put the good of the people, or country, first.

So, I traveled with all of my people, my riches, my priests and priestesses, and all of my holy symbols.

Imagine my surprise when I realized that these people were Baal worshippers, along with the king, Ahab, himself! In this little backwater town of country hicks, there was a semblance of devotion and ritual.

I immediately set about injecting some sophistication and courtly behavior into the daily life of these strange people who lived only for fighting and war with little thought of the finer things of life. The war generals schemed and sabotaged everything I tried to do. All they knew was fighting and killings and blood sacrifices to their warrior God. But I prevailed.

Not too soon after traveling to this land, I discovered something else; my husband, the King, was suffering from some form of strange depression. Periodically, he would become weak, whiny, indecisive and teary. Those periods began to last longer and longer. Finally, came the breaking point. The King decided that he wanted his neighbor, Naboth's, lettuce field.

A lettuce field!

Naboth refused to give or sell the cursed thing and Ahab sunk into a deep dark mental hole - went into his room and cried like an infant for two or three weeks! For a lettuce field! There were other lettuce fields, but he wanted that one.

A royal temper tantrum!

Finally, I went into his room to see if something could be done about this. There he was, lying on the floor, kicking and screaming, drumming his heels, and snorting like a horse!

Lord! Lord! I knew right then, my dear husband was mentally unhinged!

The people came to me saying, "Do something. Our King is teetering on the edge of insanity."

I knew I would have to take matters into my hands and run the country. My husband was simply not capable! I used intrigue, murder, and courtly deviousness to get that cursed lettuce field for him and to secure governing matters under my controls. Kings always got what they wanted.

The generals did not like a woman, a foreigner, running the country, but I kept tight control over Ahab and the army, and things were peaceful for many years.

We worshipped the gods of my people, and theirs. Those few prophets of the God, Jehovah, I had put to death. Nobody was worshipping Him anyway! Until, along came a raggedy old man named Elijah. He was constantly preaching something about my being an idolater or something!

Why would he call me an idolater? I was very faithful to my gods and goddesses.

He said he served a jealous, powerful God.

Well, so do I!

In order to keep a semblance of peace, I would have to appease him or …I tried to have him killed, but he ran away. I heard that he hid in a cave by the lake and his God sent birds to feed him. By the time my people got there, he was gone! They found nothing but bird bones and a raggedy piece of material used as a mantle. Then I heard he was living in another town with a lonely widow and her son that he mysteriously brought back to life.

Sure! Sure!

Well, he showed up again a year later and challenged me. Jehovah versus Baal.

I know you heard about that fiasco on Mt. Carmel.

Yes! I lost face and prestige, and the people doubted me and lost faith in Baal. They turned to Elijah and his God for a time after. He killed all of my priestesses and priests, my friends, and most of the house of Ahab. He then cursed me saying the dogs would lick my bones.

Why? Simply because I worshipped a different god? Or was it because I was a very strong, competent, and independent woman who ruled the country and did it very well?

The generals, in all the confusion that followed, saw their chance to rid the country of a foreign queen, me, whom they hated! They invaded my private quarters, killed my personal guards and threw me off the balcony. My dear crazy husband, the King, was killed in a battle soon after. The God of Elijah won the battle for a while, but not the war!

Remember me not as a promiscuous, empty-headed, light-skirt. Those were lies told by later writers of the Scriptures, denigrating my character because they felt threatened by my competence. Instead, remember and write what I really am. A proud, shrewd, and royal ruler, Queen and high .priestess, religious, and devoted to her god and goddess! A woman who did what she had to do, and who did it well.

What Jezebel Knows

Thoughts Create

Jezebel revealed the power of the mind in the excerpt of King Ahab, her husband. As her account unfolded, it became clear that Ahab's thoughts were all consuming. He was not able to distinguish between rational and irrational behaviors, which ultimately led to his dreadful death. Jezebel's perspective was reflected as the mind's ability to create and influence behaviors. Our thoughts impact how we respond to life and day-to-day demands.

Whether consciously or not, every person is accountable for shaping and reshaping their life. Important aspects of self-actualization are first produced by energy that later translates to thoughts and ideas that direct behavior. The role of one's unconscious mind is to consider thought. In turn, those very thoughts take form and manifest into physical and nonphysical realities.

Thoughts then, inform behaviors. What you want to bring about, you must first think about before it comes to fruition. Present realities are a reflection of inner thoughts and the meanings assigned to those ideas. If you want to alter representations of what you get, it is necessary to first change the vibration of energy needed to generate thought. You do this by simply thinking differently. Thoughts that energize and emit a heightened sense of wellbeing and "feel good" energy are at higher levels of vibration than those that evoke negative or unpleasant feelings. Mostly, this necessitates focused and deliberate energy toward thoughts you want to create, rather than attending to what you don't want. In its most organic form, *change your thoughts, impact your life.*

Identify patterns of thought that are serving you well in life and business. What can you do to protect productive patterns of thought?

Identify patterns of thought that are not serving you well in life and business. How can you interrupt unproductive thoughts?

Self-Control Rules

Jezebel didn't hold back in her expression about Ahab's mad obsession to obtain his neighbor's lettuce field. Temper tantrums and childlike fallouts characterized the king as one who lacked the ability to reason and control behaviors. There was a disregard, on several fronts, for boundaries. It became evident that the king did not consider repercussions, or simply ignored them in exchange for having what he wanted, when he wanted it. Clearly, Ahab was out of control and behaved in ways that were not conducive to a successful reign. He was emotionally erratic, self-possessive, and dismissed all aspects of willpower.

Although critical of her husband's deficiency with regards to self-monitoring, Jezebel acted in ways that were similar. Even though she appeared much more poised, her desire to have what she wanted at any cost reflected the presence of a shrewd and cunning mind. She controlled all aspects of her life and the lives of those around her. Jezebel proved, in the most horrific way, "self-preservation is knitted in self-control."

In all manner of life, self-control, or restraint, is liberating. How can restraint offer freedom? Well, consider this. Control is a semblance of security. In practicality, if you control a person, thing, or circumstance, some degree of manipulation and confinement are expected. Whatever or whomever is involved is subject to your authority, your influence, and your power. In essence, you can only trust you to get it right. A lack of trust reflects an insecurity, or uncertainty in someone or something. Self-control facilitates awareness to one's self and needs. Hence, you are free or liberated, to restrain, or control your behaviors that manifest insecurities. The ability to think and act with restraint essentially sets the human race apart from the animal kingdom. Humans have the ability to consciously process responses, thereby choosing when to and when not to react to impulses. Deliberate and calculated actions can make the difference between favorable and unfavorable impressions. Self-control involves discipline of both the mind and the body. The application of self-control ultimately leads to trust in judgment.

Pinpoint a time when you recognized that you did not exercise self-control. What were the results of your behavior? What were the lessons you learned from this experience? In reflection, do you recognize any insecurities?

Identify an area in your life where self-discipline, if exercised consistently, will benefit you and those around you?

Confidence is a Game Changer

It has been said, "Arrogance is simply untamed confidence." You will be hard pressed to find someone who does not agree that Sister Jezebel exuded bodacious confidence. By her own admission, she wore arrogance, conceit, and aggression with honor and pride. Even at the risk of losing it all, Jezebel confidently navigated through fear, and confronted anything and everything that blocked her from getting what she wanted. She demonstrated an undeniable self-assurance in who she was, what she believed as truth, and how she represented stature among the people. Jezebel was not the woman who sat and waited for a man to do anything. She had a spirit to make things happen. Authority was demanded and commanded by the very essence of her presence. No matter what, there was confidence in knowing she could count on herself. If power was king, Jezebel was surely queen.

In its simplest term, confidence may be defined as having a belief or certainty in someone or something. This can often seem elusive, fluctuating when faced with challenges and defeat. However, the ability to recognize one's core character strengths and skills is the foundation of confidence. When all else fails, this foundation on conviction builds self-esteem and an assurance of self. Operating on this sphere of self-assurance, it is easier to take risks in behaviors and emotions. It exhibits trust at the deepest level -the trust you create within yourself based on knowledge of yourself. How well do you know you? Can you rely on you when no one else will stand with you? What are your non-negotiables personally and professionally? Identify, unequivocally, your sources of reliance and strength. Consider how to tap in to your strengths and more confidently claim the sensuality of self-expression.

Think of a time when you felt bodacious confidence. How did you behave, and what were the outcomes?

In what areas of life or business would you like to show more confidence? How can you make it happen?

Chapter 3
MARY: THE MAGDALENE

The Shekinah Personified

There is no figure or character in the New Testament who is as controversial as the Magdalene woman, Mary (Miriamne). So much covering-up, deletions, and outright lies to remove this woman from her rightful place, and to denigrate her character to that of a harlot or loose woman. Her spirit literally assaulted me.

"Tell my story! Tell the truth about me. Tell of what I did. Tell them I was the beloved disciple. Tell them I was the first resurrection preacher. Tell them that I was first among the apostles…the Apostola, Apostolorum. He left me in charge of the group and gave me instructions to get them to Galilee to await the anointing of the power from on high."

On my first attempt to preach about women in ministry, and especially about the Magdalene being an apostle or messenger, the Baptist brother refused to allow me onto the pulpit. The deacon placed chairs across the front, on the floor, and indicated with a contemptuous nod of his head, that I was to preach from there. As I stood, trying to endure this insult and wanting to make a graceful exit, the members of the choir rose, came down from the choir stand, and arrayed themselves in the front pews ready to receive the message.

What a show of support! I could not leave.

The brother sat in "his" pulpit…angry, alone, and muttering while I preached, and the choir sang from the floor.

The Spirit reigned supreme that Sunday morning. I felt the divine preacher, the Magdalene, step into my soul and take control.

Question? Can we ever reconcile each other's differences and surrender ourselves to the unique harmony and oneness of the universe, or be forever caught in this eternal struggle between the God, Yahweh, and the goddess, Shekinah – Wisdom - Sophia? Both were there at the creation.

A thorough study of any aspect of history teaches that the archives are often revised or recreated to reflect the "rightness" of the oppressor or the conqueror. At the beginning of the new movement, or the people who walked in the way, the "people" consisted mainly of women, children and slaves, with a few men hanging around. It was at the ending of the first century that men began to take over and dominate the new religion with physical strength and brutality.

Women were pushed out of their positions as leaders. Their names erased from the Scriptures, their importance in Christianity downplayed, and their characters assailed, assaulted, and slandered. Jerome, in his writings of the Vulgate, called Mary Magdalene (the utmost leader), a harlot, without one shred of evidence of her promiscuity. She was too important to the narration to omit, so her character was denigrated instead. The writers changed her character, her words, and her relationship with the main character. They gave the male characters more prominence. While engaging in the required research and translation of chapters, I was convinced that the entire chapter on giving Peter the church and building properties, was added to the Scriptures for that express purpose.

Many of the books of the biblical collection were purposely lost or hidden because they gave too much headship, leadership, and prominence to the women. When one reads the Gospel of Mary, it becomes exceedingly clear that Mary was the lead apostle in the movement. Her relationship with the Savior was also clear. This gospel explored Peter's jealousy, meanness and brutality toward Mary. The Gospel of Phillip and the Gospel of Peter gave Mary prominence, intellectual superiority, and the position of companion to the Savior. According to Elaine Pagels, in her book, *Gnostic Gospels*, if one does a thorough exegesis of the Gospel of John, it becomes absolutely convincing that Mary, the beloved disciple, is the writer of the Gospel of John and the probable founder of the Johannine community. Her headship is prominent.

The Magdalene Speaks…

Yes, I was the Magdalene, Mary by name. I was the close companion (wife) of Jesus. I was the first resurrection evangelist. There was much controversy as to my race and color. I was from a small town called Magdala, near the Egyptian coast. My family was wealthy and we traveled much. I was afflicted from childhood with the scourge of epilepsy, given to sudden fits and spasms. There was no cure or remedy for this terrible thing. I was forced to endure humiliation, shame, and pity after each episode. The people said that I was demon possessed. I knew better! I knew this was simply an illness that had no known medicine to cure. My family supported me. I was educated, loved, and treated with respect.

As we traveled near the city of an obscure little town, there was much gossip in the marketplace about another itinerant preacher that had come. They were saying he was powerful, he could heal people with a "laying on of hands" or by speaking certain words. They were saying he was raising the dead, healing the sick, making the mute talk, making the lame walk, and he was giving sight to the blind! I was intrigued and my hopes flared anew. Perhaps this was worth looking into. Certainly nothing else had worked for me.

I and my women pressed our way through the crowd, my kinsmen running to keep up with us. As we got to the front of the crowd, suddenly I felt myself falling, going into a spasm, a fit, right there in the front of the crowd! I felt my feet drumming in the dust and my body stiffening into a rictus. My women were trying to hold me, to no avail. And then, through the drumming in my head, I heard a gentle yet commanding voice telling my inner self to be healed. Everything within me answered the command from that voice. A wave started at my feet and traveled throughout my body. I felt a strange sense of power coming from a hand laid on my brow. I felt an explosion in my head! Then complete quietness and peace. I opened my eyes and stared into the eyes and face of the man they were calling Jesus. He lifted me up, brushed the dust from my hair and brow, and told me I was forever healed. I tried to thank Him, but the words were lost in my tears. He lifted a corner of his robe, dried my tears and said very gently, "Walk with me." At that moment, I started my life's destiny.

My family gave me the means of survival and with their blessing, I left with Him. We walked through villages and towns preaching a message of love, salvation, and healing. We rested by riverbanks to teach, and we shared the shade of olive groves to rest our weary bodies. I, along with the other women and men who walked with us, spent hours listening to His lessons about another kingdom, salvation, and most of all, love. Many of the others, mainly Peter, resented our closeness. In fact, they were jealous of the trust and love we had between us. I was there as He struggled to accept His destiny on the cross. I cried as He cried there in the Garden of Gethsemane. At the Last Supper, I was there as He struggled urgently to impart teachings they could not grasp. I was there when they could not accept the fact that Judas and Peter would betray Him. I, alone, was able to understand his final dialogues and sermons. I was there with His mother as we stood under the cross, hearing the agonized cries, wondering in our hearts why such suffering and humiliation was required for redemption.

What redemption? Why the glorifying of shed blood and pain? Are we still trying to pacify or please a blood-thirsty and pain-loving God of the Old Testament?

Somehow, linking Eve and Adam to me and this suffering man on the cross made no sense. Was this a sorry, desperate attempt to justify the brutality of the cross? Questions! Questions! Questions!

I was there. I heard Him cry out when He felt alone and forsaken. I heard Him beg His Father to take His Spirit, that universal continuation of the Father-Son conflict. And I, alone, was there to experience the glorious resurrection of that morning. When He called my name, I felt the virtue, the strength, the power fill my being. I felt the everlasting anointing...a feeling that would never leave. When I ran to tell the men, who were in hiding, that the Savior had risen, I was excited. I was also terrified as to what it meant. I was joyful with celebration, the words were tumbling out of my mouth. He had come back to me. And to the others.

Peter, who still did not understand the meanings and teachings of Jesus, pushed me aside and called me a raving madwoman. Peter did not want to believe that He had appeared to me first, a woman (John 20: 11-18).

Go! Tell the others! He is risen!

I was the first to receive, understand, and carry the Good News. Glories upon Glories. Commissioned from the grave! Called by name, anointed, and sent with the message. Me! The bearer of the Gospel. The most important job of the apostles. The Evangeline personified. Strength, honor, and glory to my name. Education, knowledge, and writings rendered me the skills to impart the secret signs and wisdom I received from the Teacher. We woman can support ourselves with our businesses and crafts as we travel about the countryside teaching and preaching the words of the Savior. I shall tell the story to all who will listen.

What Mary the Magdalene Knows

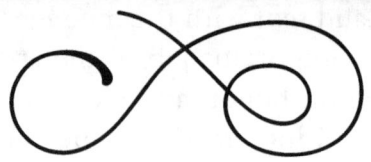

The Message is in the Messenger

Mary Magdalene had the distinct honor of being the first witness of Christ's resurrection. Here, it is important to note that during the time of this story, women were not respected as credible witnesses in the courts. Yet, the Magdalene, whose very name is translated as meaning "sin," is chosen to first validate the impossible as possible. Christ Himself commissioned her in the command, *"Do not cling to Me, for I have not yet ascended to My Father; but go to My brethren and say to them, 'I am ascending to My Father and your Father, and to My God and your God.'"* (John 20:17). Indeed, she was the first to witness divinity and eternity. It may be difficult to really imagine Mary's enthusiasm and humility as she hurried to tell the disciples and others of Christ's rising from the dead. She must have been in awe and beside herself to be comforted once more by her Lord.

Although startled at first, and hesitant, the disciples followed Mary to witness a magnificent miracle. Because of her unwavering faithfulness and evident dedication, her account seemed believable, or at least conceivable.

Of all the lessons to glean from Mary Magdalene, one of the most resounding is the ability to represent ourselves in ways that are consistent with who we say we are. No matter what you verbally communicate, your actions speak louder.

Intuition, the inner voice, has a way of uncovering truths we often would like to ignore. Usually, intuition whispers guidance that directs us towards a more authentic version of ourselves. Authenticity infers originality verified by evidence. This may be viewed as a reflection of integrity.

Integrity derives from the Latin word *integer*, meaning intact, undivided, or whole. Integrity then, is simply consistency between your inner ideologies and outer behaviors. For verification of this magnitude, one must go back to the original source. In an effort to align with your authentic self, you must identify the source of your being at the very core. It is only then that you will be able to genuinely express what you represent. Armed with this information, you can now develop insight and be able to consider the connection between your mind and your outer behaviors. Ask yourself, "Can others depend on me to be who I represent myself to be?" Now, sit still and listen to intuition.

"People with good intentions make promises — people with good character keep them"

— mediawebapps.com

How do you ensure that who you say you are aligns with your daily life and the way you do business?

What do your behaviors reveal about your most important values? What evidence do you have as a representation of this truth for you?

(Hint: Look at your calendar and your bank account summary. Generally speaking, what we value, or treasure, is indicated by where we spend time, resources, and money.)

Commitment is Glue

Mary Magdalene's response to Christ's healing of her body was one of the greatest examples of commitment. Once spared from the snares of epilepsy, she devoted herself to King Jesus. She was committed to His wellbeing and mission to save the lost. The Magdalene silently endowed to offering her best. As she led others to salvation, there was no doubt she was dedicated to the King's cause. Wherever He went, so did she. Her deep sense of gratitude was forfeit to a life of sacrifice to the most High. Once committed to following His lead, Mary was also earnest in meeting the needs of her Savior. There was an unmatched sense of dedication and representation of stick-to-itiveness.

An unwavering mind, as Mary Magdalene showed, was at the heart of her dedication. This type of commitment is different from the idea of merely showing interest. Although an interest in serving was evident in Mary's story, there was a much deeper desire to fulfill the mission she started. There was a resolve, a staying power if you will, that she allowed to dominate her soul. No matter how tough the odds became, Mary was dedicated to the will of Christ.

You have likely dedicated or committed at some point in life to someone or something. We make commitments in our daily lives with the best of intentions. We sign on to complete a project, meet a deadline, or commit to sharing ourselves or our time. At the moment of commitment, follow through seems apparent. Even possible. With little to no hesitation, we often agree to terms that later become somewhat of a burden, an imposition, or an inconvenience, that we fail to see through. Although there may be many good explanations for faltering from time to time, it would be wise to ponder, "If I were someone else, could I depend on me to be committed to the end?" Essentially the level, or degree of commitment, should be considered as well. This leads to other questions. What trade-offs may be necessary? What will I be required to do or change? In this particular instance, or situation, is the act of commitment important to me? An honest reflection may prove helpful in any determination to commit. Through a confirmation of dedication, the Magdalene gave us new insight into the phrase, *"When I commit, I don't quit."*

In what areas of life (relationships, health, personal goals, business, etc.) has the glue of commitment or dedication come undone? Be specific in your reflection.

What steps can you take to refocus your efforts in each scenario you identified?

Emotional Intelligence Keeps It Together

As you read through scenes of Mary's life, there were perhaps many occasions that warranted a push of the panic button. Yet, amid all the agony, pain, and apparent defeat she witnessed, there was a sense of peace and assurance. Unlike many other examples in the Bible, the Magdalene exhibited grace under pressure. After Christ's crucifixion, she did not run off and hide in the upper room as the disciples did. She remained steadfast. Needless to say, Mary must have experienced a certain amount of fear when she laid eyes on a man whose horrific death she had just witnessed three short days before. None-the-less, her response depicted composure. She was able to exemplify bravery in the face of uncertainty, despair, and calamity. While others ran for cover in fear of their demise, Mary stood firmly as a tree planted by a stream with roots extending deep (Jeremiah 17:8). Though she was mindful of life's retorts, she did not overthink, overdo, or overreact.

Unless one suffers from certain physical or mental disabilities, reactions are usually willfully chosen and are controllable. Those with emotional intelligence (the ability to be aware of and exercise mature emotional responses) take responsibility for circumstances and outcomes. There is an understanding of the *power of choice*. In essence, the emotionally intelligent accept responsibility for what they do, who they are, and the person they become. In practical terms, a reaction generally infers quick, and sometimes abrupt, responses. Usually this stance may appear defensive and driven purely by emotions, but the truth is, that response testifies of measured control. Although emotions are attached to responses, sound reasoning is also involved. The act of responding allows for a delay in judgment, thereby increasing the odds for a positive influence. Emotions are driven, steered by the one responding. As the roller coaster of life events call for attention, the emotionally intelligent maintains flexibility in reasoning and action. Measured responses merit intelligence.

Parallel the acts of "responding" and "reacting". When have you responded to situations, and when have you reacted? Were there differences in the results?

What impact does emotional intelligence have in your daily relationships (personal and business)?

Chapter 4
PRIESTESS OF ENDOR: THE SIBYL

Life, Meaning, and Survival

Woman is Mystique. She is mystery. She was created to be so. She holds the secrets of creation and recreation completely within her. It was ordained and made so. It was she who desired knowledge and power. Women's worship and rituals have existed since the beginning of time. As the men worship their male god of war and murder, us women will continue to worship our goddess of life…affirming life! For we bring life, nurture it, and do not have the desire to see life spilled foolishly. We revere nature and all the world that was created. We hold each blade of grass, each leaf of each tree, and each drop of water as sacred. Everything on the earth is a manifestation of the power of the divine. Blessed be.

When Yahweh made His dramatic leap into the world of men, during the trials and tribulations of the Exodus, the plagues, the burning bush, and the wandering in the desert, women's worship was already an ordained and divine fact. Sophia, Wisdom, stated in the book of Proverbs, "I was there at the beginning of creation." Because men do not understand, they do not have the knowledge, they fear us and our femininity, our woman essence, our closeness to the divine. They do not understand that to touch and smell a beautiful flower, or to feel the cool refreshing mountain stream, is to be a part of that sacredness. To bring life into the world is godly. They try to destroy us with brute force and physical oppression. They try to suppress the innate nurturing instinct, even within themselves, without realizing that during the first weeks of conception, all are female.

It seems to be the nature of man to destroy or dominate that which he does not understand. Child-bearing is a wonderful, divine mystery, a life-bringing ability given only to females, and it causes a lot of jealousy and strife among some males. They have instituted all types of rituals and symbols, trying to imitate the conception and birthing process within themselves. Some are silly methods, and some are even dangerous to life, but none have proven feasible. That gift remains forever the female's domain. They have instituted all kinds of cultural mores and laws, and have formulated religious doctrines of a jealous and spiteful God, ("for I, the Lord thy God, am a jealous God, visiting the iniquities of the fathers unto the third and fourth generations"), to control women and their bodies. That holy of holies, The Bible, has been used to keep women in subjection and submission. All females that could not be destroyed were denigrated and downgraded to worthlessness, cursed, trivialized, or mythicized. Masculinity was uplifted, placed in the image of God, or God in the image of them. Appointed to them by their own doing, the divine right to rule over women and the earth. And what a mess they have made of it.

In earlier times, women knew about the healing powers found within the earth - the roots, herbs and flowers that could cure any ailment. Men, in their greed and jealously, tried to extract knowledge from us by brutalizing, beatings and killings, ritualized torture, and annihilation. During the middle ages, or burning times, millions of women were killed and a lot of knowledge was destroyed because they dared to practice the medicinal arts and gifts of the goddess. Women were banished from the bedside and the childbirth room as male doctors took over. Midwives had to operate against the law, risking punishment and sometimes death. Knowledge of controlling conception was met harshly with death. During modern times, women have had to fight physically and emotionally against the legal and religious mores to gain control of their bodies and their reproductive systems. In their terror and fear of women, men used every method that could be found to ensure the subjection of the female within the species.

During the third century, and at the formulation of new church doctrines that featured many edicts and decrees, the theologians and church doctors spilled their hatred and vilification of women, reflecting dislike of women in their writings. Tertullian (c160-c225), the African Church Father, called women the "devil's gateway." Origen, well known for his hatred of sex and women, castrated himself at the age of eighteen to avoid the temptation of women whom he considered lower than animals.

The Priestess of Endor Speaks...

I was chosen - called by the goddess at the tender age of five. All women have power. Some, though, have an inordinate amount of the goddess's favor manifested as highly developed special abilities. I was one of those. Highly favored!

My mother and all of the women of the house saw it. I was loved, petted, adored, and shielded from the brutality of our daily lives…of warfare, and of the fears of captivity and servitude. I was especially hidden from the eyes of men, for my beauty was too much of an attraction to them. Even as a young girl, I knew the dangers of that.

When we had to leave the compound for any reason, my mother, my sisters and I, and all the other women would cover ourselves completely with layers and layers of cloth to hide our identities and our goddess-favored beauty.

I spent much of my childhood learning the divine crafts. I seemed to know instinctively what herb would cool the fevers of a fretful child; what root would help in childbirth; what seeds would aid in fertility; what leaf would staunch the flow of blood or close a wound; how to draw out the poisons of the body; what potion or infusion would knit the bones or kill pains; and which tea would put one into a deep sleep. I just knew it! I could read the weather signs with great accuracy. I could interpret dreams and omens and foretell futures. And yes, I could even speak with those in the world beyond.

My powers and gifts from the goddess surpassed my mother's and sisters' at an early age. When I reached the age of twelve, my mother and the other women took me on a pilgrimage to the sacred groves of oaks near the town of Endor, where I was dedicated as a priestess. My heart swelled with joy as I received the communion gifts of honey, milk, and the blue robes of a priestess. Since I was so young, one of the youngest ever inducted into the priesthood, I was allowed to return home and back under my mother's care until I reached my majority, or the age of eighteen. Then I would return to the grove to serve the goddess, and become a prophetic oracle for the people. My mind, my entire being, was suffused with love and adoration for her.

But, as we left the grove, I felt a premonition…a chill…. something about this place that was unsettling! One look at my mother told me she felt it too. As we left, I knew that I would return to this place one day but under very different circumstances. A picture of women fighting on horseback, and frightened children running flashed through my mind. I told my mother of these images in my head, images that would recur over the years. Even so, the next few years were good. I spent my days helping with childbirths, curing illnesses, getting more proficient in my craft, and learning proper rites, holy days of the seasons, and ceremonies of worship. I worked with the women and children. Mother would not allow me to help any man for fear they would see me, assault me, or try to bargain with my father for marriage. Still, it was fun growing up in a house of women.

When our fathers and brothers came around, we stayed quiet and out of their sight. They only wanted to talk about war, hunting, fighting, and more war. I don't think my father even knew what I looked like. He had six sons by my mother and aunts. That's all he cared about. Girls were not that important to him.

I stayed covered up around men. If one of them saw me by accident, I would fake an affliction, crossed-up eyes, and drooling lips. Once we were caught by some men at the lake. I put mud on my face and hair, rubbed stinkweed all over my arms and legs, and then chewed soap-plant. What a sight I made! Dirty, stinky, crossed-eyes and foaming at the mouth! But, I made it safely home. My mother and aunts sent us into the women's shelter if the men were drunk with wine. No man would enter a shelter. The mystery of a woman's secrets was there and they were quite afraid of it. It was our little place of refuge.

My two older sisters were married to the king, but they took their craft and their power with them. Mother made sure of that! The king and his soldiers could worship their warlike and bloody God all they wished, but we needed a Goddess of life with whom we could relate.

Word came to us that King Saul had vowed to his God to drive all goddess worshippers, (witches, they called us), from the land either by exile or by killings. Late one night, soldiers came rioting and pillaging through the towns and villages searching for the goddess marked. Many innocent women and children were raped and killed that night. But not all, for some of us had been warned in our dreams about what was coming. We had the foresight to prepare a hiding place. All of the women of our house rushed into the underground shelter and up to the caves in the mountain we had secretly prepared, and we remained there for some time until the soldiers moved on. Three of our brothers died trying to protect our household. Please, goddess. Receive their souls. They were good men who revered women and loved you.

Our mothers knew we had to leave this place; the persecutions would not stop. We needed to find a place of refuge - a safe place to live, or we would all surely die. As soon as we could go outside safely, she sent a secret message to her sisters, the warriors of the fighting women. Two weeks later, a squad of fifty, fierce, leathered, armed women rode into our compound. As my mother ran to greet them, we quickly gathered our belongings, which were already packed and waiting. And amid piled wagons and prancing horses, we left.

As we rode out of the town, other women and children came running to travel with us, offering all sorts of treasures to the warriors for protection. I could see, and my mother confirmed this, that nearly one-third of these fierce women were our kin. All of them looked like me, my sister, or my mother. The leader, the chieftain, gave me a sharp hawkish grin and said, "I am Smyrna, your aunt, your mother's sister." Another young woman, "I am Shuna, her daughter, your cousin." This went on until I had met every one of them. My heart swelled within me. I was proud to be a part of these strong, independent women. If I had not been called to the priesthood, I would surely have taken up a sword and become a warrior.

"You are truly marked by the goddess," Smyrna said. "Even more than the rest of us. We must keep you safe. We will travel to the place of the sacred oaks near the town of Endor and establish a refuge for women. The woods, caves, and rivers will offer housing and protection for all of you! And the people of the towns and villages are of like mind, so they will not betray you!" And that is what we did.

After two skirmishes with a legion of the king's soldiers who were determined to capture us, and two weeks of hot weary traveling, we rolled into the woods surrounding the town of Endor. By this time our group had more than doubled in size. We welcomed more women, men, and children seeking protection and a safe place to live. We set up shelters, cook fires, and made it our home. We established a sacred worship glade and gave thanks to the goddess for everything. Our warrior sisters guarded the woods and town until we were left in peace to worship as we pleased. Meanwhile, King Saul was still fighting. It seemed that his God told him to destroy all of the Amalekites. He said to kill them all. Even the innocent women and children, the cattle, and the grain in the fields. Saul, in a moment of lucidity, refused to kill all of them. He even saved some of the cattle, but his God became angry with him and refused to answer his prayers. Saul, desperate in the face of another war, with still another faction of crazed fighters, needed some kind of divine intervention.

His God refused to answer...petulant childlike behavior. Saul then demanded his advisors to find an oracle or prophetic woman. What irony! The very ones he had persecuted and driven into exile or killed, he then turned to for help. The wheels of the goddess of justice turned slowly but surely. He wanted the help of the women he had mocked, denied, and reviled. What a moment! What a triumph for her in whose favor I abide. Blessed be.

I called Samuel for him, who was angry at being disturbed in his sleep. Saul did not receive the answers he wished. Instead, what he heard was he would die the next day, along with his sons. What a punishment. To serve an eternally angry and wrathful God. Saul was so grateful that I had used power to help him, that he ate with me and departed in peace. Perhaps, he was reconsidering the petulant, angry reaction of his God as compared to the response of mine, and the state of his soul's resting in his coming death. Would his spirit spend eternity in the presence of chaos and wrath that seemed to surround his God? Did the clangor and confusion of battles follow one's spirit into the next life? Were warriors condemned to fight through all of eternity?

I continued to serve the goddess and affirm life until my death. Many of my fighting kinswomen, including the chieftain and my aunt Smyrna, went to a place that is now called Asia. They settled down and started a town named for her...Smyrna, (Revelations 2:8), where they built a temple and continued worship and devotion of her. Blessed be!

What the Priestess of Endor Knows

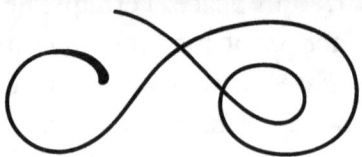

There is Power in Vision

From an early age, the Priestess, or prophet of the gods, possessed an ability to see things that were not present. Although she lived physically within the bounds of the immediate, her mind elevated her to places that others couldn't imagine. The Priestess of Endor casted a vision for her life and the lives of others, far into the future. There was clarity and detail in her accounts. She was able to recognize, innately sense, change and respond to the forthcoming. Because the Priestess could see that which was unseen, she was able to articulate the far-reaching effects of expectancy.

There is power in vision. Unlike physical sight, vision commands a more compelling view, buried in the depth of the soul. Whereas sight is operative of the eyes, vision is operative of the heart. In many ways, vision is the mind's eye. It is an opening to the bowels of hope and possibilities. Greatness dwells in vision. Nothing formed has ever been done without the presence of vision. Vision shapes creativity. Inwardly stored, yet outwardly projected, vision guides destiny.

Generally, when acting in the present, you can only see that which is present. Hence, there are limitations, in a sense, to what you do because you are acting based upon limited feedback. The absence of foresight restricts the ability to look beyond the immediate. Vision, however, stretches the portals of insight. Those who have mastered the ability to operate in the present based on what is possible a year from now, ten years from now, or even a generation from now, understand the wealth that resides in vision. Vison compels you to act when there is little to no evidence of momentum. There is an assuredness that there will be an affect - an impact that will inevitably be revealed. Vision demands reliance upon a belief that what you do now will make a difference in the future. Vision, the scope of what you see, can be measured by your actions today. Check your vision. Are you nearsighted or farsighted?

What is the bigger picture you see for your life (relationships, health, finances, career, spiritual, social). Write a *Vision Statement* that reflects your life 10-30 years into the future. See an example of a Vision Statement in Appendix B.

What behaviors can you adjust now that will move you closer to your envisioned life?

Take Your Powers with You

The Priestess of Endor saw herself, and other women, differently than she was viewed by the men. Threatened by persecution and death, she and others took refuge in woody areas. There, they set up camp as they tried to survive as best as they could. Though uprooted and forced to abandon their homeland, the priestesses did not forsake what they represented. Instead, they fostered an even stronger self. No matter what happened or what foreign land they found, there was a commitment to allow the overriding powers of nature within themselves to flow freely. There was no parting of the special powers the priestesses possessed; it was the essence of their existence. The environment or atmosphere may have been different, however the presence of power, the thing that helped define who they were, remained the same. The Priestess of Endor substantiated the premise of separation by death only.

Unlike the priestesses, often when meeting new challenges or confronted with the unknown, we forget the powers within. Unique instinctual abilities and those gained along life's path shift when you shift. It doesn't matter where you go, you will ultimately show up. There is no separation between your inner and outer you. End of story. From this perspective, who you are is far more valuable than where you are. There are powers that reside within you, at the deepest spheres, that only you can detect and access. These powers act as a North Star, guiding your every thought, idea, belief, value, and state of being. The same power that resurrected Christ from the tomb; the power that called Lazarus from the dead; the healing power that flowed through the woman with the issue of blood, is the same supernatural power that rests in you. How do I know this to be true? Romans 8:11 offers confidence in this matter.

"But if the Spirit of Him who raised Jesus from the dead dwells in you, He who raised Christ from the dead will also give life to your mortal bodies through His Spirit who dwells in you."

Awareness of power in Spirit is critical; it heightens your senses.

"And the Lord God formed man of the dust of the ground, and breathed into his nostrils the breath of life, and man became a living being."

Genesis 1:7

How you define yourself is often the difference between aimlessly wandering and miraculously arriving.

How do you define YOU? Create a *Self-Definition Statement*. See an example in Appendix C.

Consult with five of your closest confidants. What are three to five adjectives consistently used to describe you?

Daily Habits Determine Results

The Priestess of Endor established a routine, a daily practice, when in the company of the drunken men. There was no question as to what she needed to do when certain events were occurring. The young women were taught to protect themselves and to recognize imminent danger. They practiced an 'if this – then that' way of life, living with contingencies. In other words, the men's behaviors determined the appropriate action they took. There was a constant dance of initiated action and a subsequent response to that action. Daily habits prepared the women for survival among the presence of evil.

Daily habits impact potential outcomes. My high school coach would often say, "What you do on the practice field shows up in the game." This being the case, my daily habits determined my results. Scientific perspectives explain the concept of habit forming. Repetitive behaviors are eventually, over time, engrained into the neuropaths of the brain. Patterning, or routine, becomes somewhat automatic. Daily routine is really practice that helps to establish longer lasting behaviors. In short, routines are strengthened when consistently repeated. The structure you create in the brain cemented by habitual actions replaces the need for motivation. Once your life, your brain, is programmed or structured with familiarity, you eliminate indecisiveness and the necessity for external rewards. An internal drive takes control, guiding from the subconscious realm. Whether you choose negative habits or positive ones, you are gaining momentum towards the manifestation of something greater in expansion.

"Chains of habit are too light to be felt until they are too heavy to be broken."

Warren Buffet
Investor and Philanthropist

List daily habits or routines in at least three key areas of your life. What are the results because of these habits/routines?

What habits or routines can you implement that will impact your life and/or business for the better?

Chapter 5
DEBORAH: THE GENERAL JUDGE

Prophesy, Sing, and Fight

While preparing a sermon for Sunday Service, I was deep into the study of the Old Testament judges, prophets, and war leaders. The phrase, "and they did evil in the sight of the Lord," repeated itself over and over.

What sin? Worship other gods? What evil did they continually commit, other than killing each other in senseless fighting? Is it relevant to today's troubles and evils? Were those wars, skirmishes, takeovers, murders, child killings, and spouse killers a foreshadowing of what we have now become? Are the wars we fight in the name of freedom and democracy justified by scripture? Are we serving a blood thirsty, wrathful God who regularly requires sacrifices in the fields of fighting to expunge some sins…sacrifices of the innocents in great numbers? Or, is it the brutish, carnal, selfish nature of us all, given to eternal fighting and taking? Have we made ourselves a God in our own image? A reason to continually fight and kill in the name of a tribal god who neither sees nor cares? Maybe, we are forever created, caught, and used by two powerful and ancient entities, Yahweh and Baal.

Fighting, warfare, trickery, and deceit, began in the opening books of the Old Testament Scriptures and carried through to the end of the closing book of the New Testament. The inter-testament Scriptures bridged the span between the two with still more fighting and warfare. Does the tribal male god, Jehovah of the patriarchal Israelites, continue to be in competition with the goddess, or the women's Deity, Ashtoreth, or Queen of Heaven?

Jeremiah wrote in his ranting and ravings to the tribe of Dan in the seventh chapter, "The children gather wood, and the fathers kindle the fire, and the women knead their dough, to make cakes to the Queen of Heaven, and to pour out drink offerings unto other gods." And yet, with all of his weeping, the Queen of Heaven had not been defeated. Perhaps, even now, she sits above, watching the eternal struggle. Even with harsh threats of vile punishments, the people of Dan continued to worship her, along with the women of the other tribes. Saul, in his reign of terror, had many of her priestesses and women of power killed or exiled. What irony that the very thing he tried to eradicate, women's worship rituals, was what he searched for in his hour of desperate need. The Priestess of Endor displayed extraordinary power, even in fear for her life.

As I read of the continued warfare between the tribes themselves and with the Canaanites, I found more questions. Why would an all-powerful God send his people to take the land already occupied by another people? Send them with the command to kill every woman, man and child, causing strife that is still played out today? Across the centuries, how many innocents have been slaughtered because some desired the belongings of another? How many wars have been fought because of greed and jealousy, couched and hidden in words of piety and religion? Even today there are questions. Is a theocracy always one of fighting, oppression, fractious politics, territorial egomania, and brutality in the name of a jealous God? Was Deborah, a woman of wealth, influence, prophetic power, and strategic and military might, used for peace or politics? Was Deborah and Jael of the legendary Amazons?

Yes.

Was Deborah really a Jew as some claimed?

No.

Is this not Jael's story?

Yes.

And who was Lapidoth? Her name translates not as husband but as the Torch Woman, light bearer, or perhaps her lover and close friend?

Questions that each reader must answer for him or herself.

Deborah the Judge, the Warrior, the Prophet Speaks…

I am Deborah. I have with me, my tribal sister, Jael. Although we were not part of their tribes, we were affiliated with the Tribe of Dan. Also with me was my torch woman, Lapidoth. We were fighting, fierce warriors, who worshipped the same goddess and gods of Dan's tribe. In fact, many of their women joined our fighting squads. Those women made strong fighters. Our lands were joined, and we lived in peace with each other.

The prophet, Jeremiah, came to our land preaching and threatening all manner of punishment if we continued to worship the Queen of Heaven. He did not want the people of Dan to declare a holiday, make cakes, decorate their houses, or sing and dance in her honor. He said it was an affront to his God Jehovah. He claimed it was also wrong to have women as chiefs, leaders, and fighters. Was it not enough that they had invaded our country, but did they also have to enforce their bloody God, their strange beliefs, and their constant fighting on us?

I was a judge because of my military might and prophetic gift. You might call me an oracle. I had a special place on my vast land holdings, a group of palm trees, and a rather large lake - an oasis. I liked to sit there in the coolness and dispense civil rulings and judgments. People from all over came to me to settle their disputes.

The Israelite tribes had been at war with the Canaanites for years. They invaded these lands, and the Canaanites were still trying to drive them and their one, God thing out. Now the Israelites cried out to their God Jehovah for deliverance from an imminent attack by yet another invader, Jabin, and his mighty iron chariots. I sent for Barak, the commander of the army. I told him what should be done to hold back the assault because an assault on the lands of Dan would also put my lands in danger.

Strategically, Dan's lands, the towns, and cities of Laisch, were the first lines of defense. Jael was fighting because the Kenites had already laid claim to her lands. But Barak was afraid and intimidated by the might of Jabin and Sisera's army. He refused to go, even if his God commanded it. Finally, after much prompting and assurance from me, he agreed to go if my warriors and I would go with him. Our fame as a fighting force had spread far and wide. I said to him, "If I go with you and we win, the victory will go to a woman." I had seen (in a vision) the part my sister Jael would play in this battle. Barak did not care who the war went to as long as he got some help and got out alive.

The night before the battle, Barak was in deep contemplation, questioning his part in this never ending fight for god knows whatever reasons. Why the constant fighting, maiming and dying for a piece of land, jewels, or simply because some jealous God said fight and kill? Where is the reverence for life, appreciation for the finer things, peace, and all of those things that make life worthwhile? Things the goddess represented? Things the men have no regard for in their continuous struggle for dominance?

Well, I went with Barak and the battle was won. In all of the struggle and melee, Sisera jumped out of his chariot, sloughed through the mud, and ran away to the tents of the Kenites. He met Jael, the ferocious warrior, and her women, coming to fight him. But Sisera was exhausted, worn out from fighting and running. This was not a worthy challenge to Jael, not even worth the effort.

Sisera couldn't even stand. Jael knew she would have to confront him in a different way. After all, he did not deserve the honor of dying by the sword because of his cowardly action of running from the field and deserting his men.

Some writers have tried to portray Jael as a docile wife of Heber, sitting in the tents with other docile women waiting for captivity. It is not true. When Barak came running to kill Sisera, it was already done. Jael struck the deciding blow. Sisera died by her hands. The victory went to Jael. Blessed above women shall Jael be. Blessed shall she be above women (Judges 5:24). We will sing the praises continually of this woman. Hosannas to the mighty Jael! She will go back to ruling the lands of the Kenites that she occupied before this invasion (Judges 5:6).

My sister was indeed a mighty woman and a great warrior. She had secured peace for this fractured land. I will write a song for this day, to those who stood with me, Barak and Jael. I will write for the tribes who stood and fought. Yes, even I, Deborah, the mighty fighter, will sing to the honor of this battle. I will extol even those that did not help their kinsmen. This day, your God has won the battle. Another day, perhaps other gods will triumph.

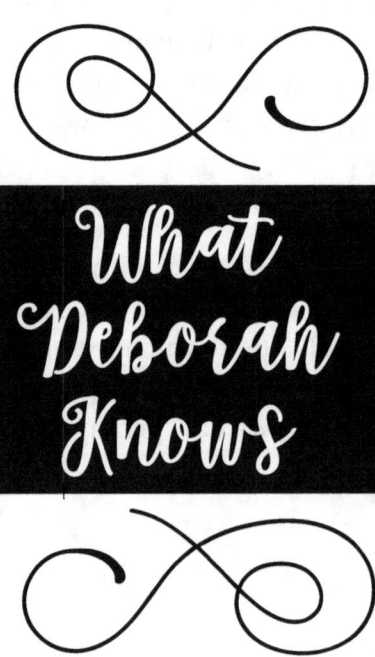

Networks Net Survival

There is force in numbers. Deborah surrounded herself with other women who were mighty, fierce, and focused. She and her band were leaders to be reckoned with, took nothing for granted, and were always watchful. As a judge, prophetess, warrior, ruler, and poetess, Deborah was skilled in connecting with allies and establishing ties. She artfully identified resources and strengths within each and every comrade, and calculated how she might be able to join forces that would result in triumph. Deborah shared all that she had and all that she was for the sake of pushing her agenda, and that of others.

Connecting is about your ability to engage with others and offer value. Rewarding relationships impact fulfillment, wealth, and achievement. When you identify ways to enrich the lives of others and begin to promote their agenda, no strings attached, you add value. By most accounts, this kind of act is rare. Most tend to do the least or exert the least effort, while expecting to gain highly in return. Simply, most relationships are formed between parties who seek something from others in the connection. There is rarely an act of giving, without the expectation of receiving in return. However, value infused comrades tend to reciprocate. Connecting, or networking with others in this way multiplies energy. Energy multiplied creates synergy. Through synergy, the individual efforts of all parties are combined to render greater impact than would have been generated by individual efforts. You've heard the old adage, *"You can't give what you don't have."* When we feel valued, we are at liberty to be our best selves. There is an aurora of goodness, kindness, and confidence released in the transaction that trades value for value.

How have you added value to those who are connected to you?

How have your connections helped you in business or in your personal life?

Fight with Everything within You

As a warrior, Deborah was brilliant, strategic, and by some accounts, a Wonder Woman. Savvy with words and the sword, she could easily cut an enemy with her tongue or her blade. Equipped to carry out the charge, Deborah bravely led an army of ten thousand to victory over an army of on hundred thousand. Heralded as a heroine, she was portrayed in the Bible as a fearless fighter who aided Barak, a male leader in Israel's army.

No doubt, there are some battles in life that call for an all-out whooping. You know what I mean – remove the earrings, kick off the shoes, and roll up the sleeves kind of fight. What Deborah knew was that dogmatic determination gets the prize. In effect, life happens to all of us. There are times of joy, times of sorrow, times of defeat, and times of triumph. The real question is, can you be affected but not infected? We live in a world of polar opposites. As you move forward, there is always a force pushing back in some form, whether physically, emotionally, or spiritually. In these moments, there is no time to waver, ponder, or halt. You have to go all in, no holds barred, just dig in and fight!

There is something magnificent to be said about a person who was able to stare down the barrel of what seemed impossible and yet remain undeterred. The person who has a deep-rooted passion to never give up will ultimately be rewarded. The greatest reward comes in the form of contentment, a peace that passes all understanding. When you live life all in, or as they say in basketball, "full court press," on purpose and in purpose, there are no regrets. I believe a sense of significance and fulfillment prevail. Paul gives us a glimpse of this endearment in 2 Timothy 4:7.

> *"I have fought the good fight, I have finished the race, I have kept the faith."*

In the end, when there is no doubt you gave it all you had to give, you can throw in the towel and walk away empowered. Fight with everything within you. You have the ability to win both the battle and the war.

Identify an area where you could use more dogmatic determination. What do you think the outcome would be if you actually committed wholeheartedly to engage in the fight?

Reflect on a time when you showed dogmatic determination. Close your eyes. Recall the feeling of determination. What do you notice happening in your physical body? What emotions come through in this moment?

Promote Yourself

Deborah was a woman who wore many hats. She was a judge, songwriter,, warrior, political leader, and given many other roles and responsibilities. No matter how stretched she was, her nature was one of striving for excellence in everything she did. Her agenda was to fulfil a legacy. Sometimes this task involved others, and sometimes not. The ultimate goal was to get the job done, taking full responsibility for the grind, and the outcomes.

One of the most noble ways to promote yourself is to carry out the tasks you enlist and fill the roles in which you serve. Have you ever heard someone say, "That's not my job?" Or what about, "I wasn't hired to do that." The persons who make such statements fail to take advantage of opportunities. Thomas Edison is credited with stating, "*Opportunity is missed by most people because it is dressed in overalls and looks like work."* The opportunist realizes work often equates to experience. However, let me be clear; involvement in the same task, assignment, or role for the past ten years is a single experience that is played out over a ten-year span. It is not ten years of experience. On the contrary, experience that promotes is perpetuated by variance, or change over a period of time. In other words, you are exposed to and accept new and different challenges. More often, these new and different challenges are outside the confines of your usual responsibilities. Norms of familiarity are extended beyond the bounds of comfort zones. In turn, these new experiences provide a platform to negotiate position and income.

When you reflect an attitude that causes you to show up, learn, and actively participate in moving goals forward within and outside of your usual assignment or role, you simultaneously promote yourself to the front of the line. Colossians 3:23 admonishes us, *"And whatever you do, do it heartily, as to the Lord and not to men."* As Deborah modeled for us, there is no need to call attention to self or undermine anyone else in the process. Promotion comes through activity. Knowing what to do, when to do it, and how to do it makes you invaluable. As The Stimuknowlogy Institute shares, whether in your personal or professional life, when you choose to *"work for excellence rather than a paycheck,"* a promotion is inevitable.

What would activity look like if you were choosing to promote yourself in your path?

How does "working for excellence" differ from "working for a paycheck?"

Chapter 6
THECLA: THE PREACHER

Guardian Lions and the Word

A new woman who spoke to my spirit was Thecla, a dynamic preacher of the first century in this new religion called Christianity. The lands and regions were in the turbulent grips of many major religions, all fighting for dominance. The Roman males gave complete allegiance to the warrior god Mithra, that was part bull. The Roman women were being inducted to serve as vestal virgins in the houses of various goddesses. The Greeks were devout in their service to the gods and goddesses of Mt. Olympus and their philosophers. The Babylonians had their mystery religion. The Egyptians were still enthralled with the Pharaohs and their hieroglyphical scriptures of the dead, and their sexual exploits in the afterlife. And, there were many smaller representations of paganism and polytheism. In this morass of "isms," schisms, and philosophies, Christianity had to fight for recognition and the prevention of complete absorption by other belief systems.

Instead, Christianity took on the symbols and dogmas of several religions and repackaged them as one complete set of spiritual beliefs. Mithra and the sacrificial blood of the bull on the scaffold, "covered in the blood," was changed into the sacrifice of the Christ on the cross and the regenerative power of the shed, covering blood. The Trinity moved from queen, consort, and child, to Father, mother, and child, and finally to Father, Son and Holy Ghost. The Mother Goddess or the Shekinah, became the hidden, deleted, or invisible part of the Godhead. The Goddess, Queen of

Heaven, became Mary the mortal, perpetual virgin. Also known as the theotokos, or bearer of god, she was later re-named the deified Co-Redemptrix. The young maiden became the exalted virgin and the goddess, Wisdom, was brought down to "logos," then to Jesus.

During this turbulent time, there were many itinerant preachers, prophets, soothsayers, philosophers, and sorcerers, all intent on exhorting their own brand of religion and denigrating the others. The Christian Apologists were busy for a lifetime defending their made-up doctrines and dogmas which had a true flavor of myth, legend, and fairytale. Itinerant preachers wandered the countryside exhorting their beliefs. Men and women were fanatic and zealous in their devotions and knowledge that they had received the true Word of God. After the bloody and chaotic establishment of the "Christian church" as an institution, men began the brutal eradication and removal of women from leadership roles within the church. Their names were deleted from the Scriptures and their stories reduced to romantic fairytales. The stories of the trinity were re-written, placing the female presence in the nameless position of a ghost. After an inordinate amount of bloodshed and strife, the reins of the church were firmly in the grip of egotistical, power-hunger, dogmatic men called Church Fathers and Doctors. The Church Mothers' words and writings had been eliminated, hidden or completely deleted. Women such as Theodosia, Maximilla, Priscilla, Theresa, Veronica, Thecla, Huldah Catherine, Julian, Macrina, Monica, Hilda, and the Magdalene were a distant memory.

The ecumenical council of bishops, all male, stated it was unseemly and ungodly for a young woman to travel about the countryside preaching, unaccompanied by a male in authority. Furthermore, she was too much in competition with Paul. How dare she call herself a preacher and be compared to Paul! I felt compelled to find Thecla, travel in her footsteps, find her shrine, and reclaim her as a preaching sister in the Scriptures. All glory given, Thecla found me. Books appeared as if by magic. Information came from everywhere, and lastly, as I entered the home of a dear friend, now departed, there on her wall was a very large picture of the beautiful Thecla and her guardian lion. I greeted her.

"Hello Thecla!"

I felt in my spirit that my search had finally reached fruition. After a thorough examination of the Scriptures, Acts of Paul and Thecla, and the exegesis of Ecclesiastical history by a New Eusebius, I found this passage recorded by Tertullian, an early Christian author.

"She (Thecla) was reported to be a convert, belonging to the district of Iconium and Antioch, and became a Christian Teacher, Preacher, and Baptizer."

Thecla was also given the titles "The Illuminator," the Light Bringer, the Truth Speaker. Churches and shrines dedicated and named after Thecla are still found in Asia today.

Welcome back Thecla, step forth and retake your rightful place among the preaching women of the church. Stand with Chloe, Nympha, Prisca, Phoebe, the Woman at the Well, and the dynamic Magdalene. Her spirit calls. I must go to Antioch.

Thecla Speaks…

I am Thecla, daughter of a very wealthy Greek family. I was educated, schooled in the fine arts and some sciences. On a certain day, I was trying on my wedding gown. My maids were excited, my family was pleased. I was marrying the son of another wealthy family. No love there, just obedience to family. The windows were opened to catch the cool summer breeze when all of a sudden I heard the voice of someone expounding. Preaching. Nothing unusual about that…someone was always out there yelling about one god or another. I stepped to the window and looked out. There, standing between the columns of the Temple of Diana, was a misshapen older man speaking a strange doctrine about a Savior who died for our sins.

What Savior? What sins? A crucifixion and a resurrection? What nonsense was this? Everyone knew the Romans crucified criminals all the time. Nothing holy or mysterious about that. But they did not come back to life.

I wanted to know more.

I sat down in the window sill to listen and became mesmerized by the conviction I heard in his words. Words about salvation and grace and a supernatural man actually coming back to life and appearing to his friends. There was a promise, the coming of another kingdom. This was very different than our relationships with the gods on Mt. Olympus, in Hades, or even the philosophers who taught on the benches. Every day he came to the Temple of Diana to preach and every day I listened for hours. I listened for as long as he preached.

Finally I decided to go down into the street to be closer and to hear more. My family went crazy. They thought I had lost my mind or become possessed by demons. They imprisoned me in the rooms of the house, but I bribed my maids and escaped. Down to the streets, I ran. This Savior was calling me! I felt the urging and compulsion deep within my very soul. I had to go! Wedding plans, family wishes, everything was forgotten. I had to go!

I walked the streets for days with the group that surrounded the preacher. After the preaching all day, we would sit around the fire at night for teaching. Paul recognized my pointed, probing, insightful questions, and knew I was destined to preach the Word. He knew I had been called.

One day, I felt a force, an essence, or something, fall on me and I began to preach. The words were falling out of my mouth. I could not stop. I was in the grip of something powerful! I preached for hours until finally I felt a loosening, an easing of the force. I collapsed in total exhaustion and was carried from the street to a safe place.

My family and my fiancé found me one day, preaching in the market place, and threatened to kill me if I did not return home. I refused to go and was thrown in jail. Sometime in the night, I heard a voice constantly saying to me, "I will never leave you nor forsake you." I felt that presence wrap around me, keeping me safe. Several of the guards came to stare at me, but they never touched me; they just looked and walked away. I was taken to court along with Paul. My mother screeched at the judge to burn me at the stake as an example to other young women who wished to forsake all that was seemly to run towards some trumped up religion. They marched me out to the city square (the burning place), tied me to the pole, and set me afire. As the flames began to lap and scorch my clothes and smoke filled my nostrils, I prayed fervently for a quick mortal release. From out of nowhere a black rain cloud, fat with moisture, hovered over me and let down its heavy load of water. The fire went out immediately. I turned my face up to receive this blessing of the Holy One.

All of the women in the crowd screamed for my release and rushed forward to touch me, to receive a blessing or just a small sprinkle of that water. The guards were astonished and did not know what to do with me so they carted me back to jail. After leaving the jail two days later, I was forced to go to my home, where I stayed until late that night. I collected my money, a lot of it, some jewelry, my warmest cloak, sturdiest shoes, and quietly left by the window. I took my two maids with me and rejoined the preaching band. We moved from town to town, countryside to riverbank, and dusty desert to arid mountainside. I preached, taught, healed, and wrote alongside Paul for many months, until I felt the Spirit urging me to go out from among them.

Paul had repeatedly refused to baptize me, but the Spirit said I had greater work to do. I knew with every fiber within me that the Holy One would be my protection. I left the group and set out on my own. Several of the band members decided to go with me, which caused much anger and strife. One day, my followers and I were walking along a dusty trail. We were hot, tired and very thirsty, but there was no water in sight. Our water skins were dry. Would we die of thirst here along this trail? I crawled over to a big pile of rocks and began to pray. I was so deep in that prayer, it took some time for me to notice that my fingertips were feeling damp. I looked, and there in the dirt and dust, a small but steady stream of water was pooling at my hand. We shouted in amazement and gave prayerful thanks. We drank and slurped that cool, healing, and refreshing water until our thirst was truly quenched and our souls revived! We rested in that place for many days. The water kept coming up out of the ground and trickling down through the cracks of the big rocks and boulders, spreading out and making a small lake. A shrine in my honor, St. Thecla, is still there. Again, the Holy One taking care of me.

Once more, we were traveling and preaching along the roadside, and I was separated from the rest of the group. One of the rich merchants of the city attempted to seduce me, and because of my vows of celibacy and chastity, I rebuffed him. In his anger, shame, and humiliation, he assaulted me. I fought back and tore his expensive clothes. After spending a night in the dungeons, we were marched out onto the hot sands of the coliseum. We were standing there in a tight little group when the crowd began to roar and scream. Not for us, but for the lions that had entered the arena. We began to run and scatter to the four corners of the arena. Some were screaming as the lions pounced and tore into them. I braced myself against the wall and began to pray, not for deliverance, but for strength and endurance, and the steadfastness and courage needed to endure this. I prayed that my faith would hold to the end of my trial. When I opened my eyes, there were two lions coming towards me, and I trembled as I prepared to die. Just as the lions pounced, out of nowhere a huge lioness jumped in front of me, pushing them back. She guarded me. She paced back and forth in front of me, allowing no other lion to get to me. Neither would she allow me to move from that space. I remained there while the grisly, gory spectacle continued until I was the only one left on the sands. As I walked to the center of the field, with the lioness at my side, the crowd screamed for my release. However, the Ruler was not ready to see me go.

As I stood there, I saw a vat of water - an unusual sight considering the value placed on water (there wasn't much to go around in the desert). Since Paul had refused to baptize me I would do it for myself. I felt an anointing fall on me again. I walked over and jumped in the water to cover myself with this life giving liquid. I remained there, splashing around and completely immersing myself. It was only later that I saw the predatory sharks that had jumped out of the vat and onto the sand when I got in. The other lions turned and ate them instead of me. The crowd was almost out of control. They wanted to see me released. As I stood there on the excruciatingly hot sand, with the lioness, my self-appointed guardian, the Ruler's wife, Tryphena, left her box, came to the edge of her balcony, and beckoned to me. She threw down her gold-embroidered leather sandals to me, her thin silk outer wrap, and her velvet coin purse, heavy with metal pieces of money. She turned to her husband and said in a loud voice, "This woman is touched by the Divine. Let her go!" She then turned and left the stadium.

Other women started throwing money and silks down to me. They screamed and cheered as I walked around picking them up, with my guardian following closely behind me. As the guards escorted me back to the pens with my gifts and my lioness, who would not leave my side, the crowds erupted again with cries for my freedom! I sat quietly in the pens for the rest of the day, shaded from the sun and the noise. Only the occasional chuffing of my lion interrupted the quietness. At evening tide the guards cautiously approached me and said I was free to leave. It seemed that the governor had been besieged all throughout the day by a large crowd of influential women, including his wife, who demanded my freedom.

The guard handed me a leather sack and a skin of water, then guided me to the gates. As I left the city, a carriage pulled up. It was the Ruler's wife. She navigated the crowd of women surrounding me, came up and stated that she would walk a short distance with me. She asked questions concerning my beliefs and my faith, and I knew right then that her heart was being cleansed and converted. Here would stand another disciple, a true believer, perhaps another preacher of the Word. We stopped beside the river and I immediately baptized her and several others who would be my followers and members of my preaching band. My guardian continued with me always. She was my warmth in the cold desert night, brought food when I was hungry, and always, unerringly, found water. A gift from the Holy One. I preached, taught and traveled for many years, always under the unction and guidance of that protective Spirit. When my body became too frail for traveling, I retreated to a cave in the mountains with my guardian to write and teach those who came to learn of the One I served.

Find my Scriptures! Find my written words! Remember me always as Thecla and the Lion…preacher and teacher renown.

What Thecla Knows

Question Your Questions

As Thecla adorned herself in preparation for her wedding day, she was intrigued by a gentleman who spattered a message that didn't seem to make sense. Instead of dismissing the rattle as nonsense, she listened even more carefully and began to reason with the old man's speculations. Her core was struck with a vast cord of curiosity. There certainly was something that she deemed important enough to attempt to unscramble the puzzling words.

I was told if I asked quality questions, I would get quality answers. Thecla certainly engaged this very act of speculation. So, exactly what are quality questions? Here, the term "quality" infers exploration. Thus, quality questions and statements prompt curiosity. For example, statements or questions like "I wonder," "I imagine," "If this, then that may be possible," "Is there a possibility no one else has contrived?," or, "What do you think might happen?" denote curiosity. Quality questions and statements open pathways to possibilities, and are usually open-ended. The brain will search for information to fill in the gaps between what you know and what you seek to know. From a neuroscientific perspective, this is called firing of the reticular activating system (RAS).

What is this RAS? Have you ever wanted something so badly you could hardly stop thinking about it? Let's take for example, a particular type of car. The latest version of that E500 Mercedes caught your eye, and you couldn't shake the idea of being seated in one of those beauties. You haven't decided to purchase the vehicle, but all of a sudden everywhere you look, there seems to be an E500. Because you imprinted the desire, or curiosity to own the car into your brain, the organism now searches, subconsciously and consciously, to find the vehicle in this example. Similar to the brain's ability to scan the environment to find the car, it has the capacity to search for answers to questions you pose, especially those arousing curiosity. As you begin to question questions daily, consider whether you are probing on the surface or extending to the unknowns. Curiosity sparks innovation and creativity. In this regard, the walls of possibility are expanded, as there is a willingness to veer from the beaten paths. Like Thecla, when you reach into the depths of wonder, you will often be amazed.

"Imagination is more important than knowledge. For knowledge is limited to all we now know and understand, while imagination embraces the entire world, and all there ever will be to know and understand."

*— **Albert Einstein***
Theoretical Physicist

Think of a problem or something that you want to be made clearer. Pose quality and curious questions to the universe. How can you debunk the impossible, or the "It's never been done that way" statement?

Close your eyes. Imagine your ideal life. What do you hear, feel, smell? Indulge all your sense, slowly breathing in through your nostrils and out through your mouth. Bask in imagination. Note your experience.

Lead Passion Passionately

Thecla laid everything, all of her possessions, her family, future treasures, and reputation on the line, in order to follow the pull she felt in her spirit. She did not sit for weeks, months, or years pondering whether she had clear directions, resources, or support. The girl just knew there was a force within that propelled her. The tug was too forceful to ignore. Absent a business plan or blueprint, Thecla scaled the walls of mediocrity and was thrusted into a life of significance.

Over and over again, I've heard the advice, "Follow your passion." To some degree, I agree with this take. However, Thecla offered a different spin to the idea. As a contemporary role model, she would likely advise you to move in the direction you are pulled and make way for passion to follow you. Why should passion lead if you're the one driving your goals and dreams? When you lead passion, you may not necessarily go in the direction the masses dictate or expect. You may not follow the path of least resistance, or strike out into familiar territory. To lead with passion, Thecla had to sit still and curiously listen. She was open-minded, willing to take both calculated and uncalculated risks. She didn't go on some long retreat or enlist thoughts from long lost friends. Instead, Thecla purposely placed herself in the midst of the pull, even though she didn't have all of the answers or instructions.

There may be times when you vigorously want something or want to pursue something new or different. Often, to our surprise, that which we so feverishly desire may not be the pull that quietly attempts to lead to new ground. It is especially important to slow life's pace during these moments. If not, you risk the dismissal of a blessing by slamming the door shut in the face of opportunity. Quiet, gentle whispers are purposed this way. In order to decipher the cues, you must sit, rest, meditate. Once cleared, with every fiber of enthusiasm, plunge from the mount of faith.

Recall Proverbs 3: 5-6.

"Trust in the Lord with all your heart, And lean not on your own understanding; In all your ways acknowledge Him, and He shall direct your paths."

As Thecla revealed, when you listen to the tug, explore, and respond, the resources will follow. Lead passion passionately and witness awe and wonder.

Consider a time when you led passion, instead of allowing passion to lead you. What was the tug? What were the results?

How can you infuse passion into a project, relationship, business venture, or an area of life where you aren't necessarily excited, but know that you will reap greater rewards if you do so?

First In, First Out

Thriving leadership recommends leading by example. Thecla certainly heeded this advice as she demonstrated leadership by followership. It became apparent rather quickly that Thecla had been called to serve in a significant capacity alongside Paul. She heard a calling and responded with zeal. Leaving all that she owned or ever dreamed to own behind, she enlisted as a follower to show her commitment to learning and service. Because of her decision, she was deemed rebellious and thus chased by her family and the rulers of the country in attempts to eradicate her. No matter the attacks, she thrived and remained an example of leadership through her tenacious acts of preaching and teaching. Other women in the land adored her and made attempts to protect her life, even at the risk of losing their own. Because of her conviction, she was able to lead in a way that drew others to her side as loyal followers. Her life became an example for others to fearlessly follow, and with much resolve.

Thecla was the first in and the first out when she chose to lead by example. She went into Paul's camp with many riches and came out stripped of worldly possessions - a lesson for her soon to be followers.

Thecla's acts remind us to take a closer look at ourselves and question motives and behaviors. Why you do something will largely determine how you do it. If you commit to a task begrudgingly, you will likely work through it begrudgingly. If you take on a new challenge with excitement, you will likely approach resolutions positively. As T. Harv Eker said, *"How you do anything is how you do everything."* In order to lead by example and with authenticity, you must first be willing to lead yourself, especially in areas that may be difficult to face. When you question motives and behaviors, you are offered an opportunity to get laser clear on both intentions and purpose. The greatest act of leadership is taking the lead from within.

Check your motives over the next several days. Why are you doing what you choose to do for someone else, and/or for yourself? Once you uncover motives, consider what this says about the person you are, or are becoming.

Leadership suggests that we take control of our lives before asking others to follow. Identify an area in your life where improvement on self-leadership will benefit you the most.

Chapter 7
RAHAB: THE BUSINESS WOMAN RENOWN

The story of this indomitable, cunning, shrewd and intelligent woman took place against a background of deceit, cruelty, and war. But amidst that, Rahab was a survivor, a business woman, a caretaker, and a woman with absolute faith in her abilities as an independent and wealthy individual.

Rahab was not a harlot, as early church writers would have us believe. All research shows that she was an astute and able business woman. She was the Innkeeper of her own building on the wall, a prime piece of property. Rahab was also a weaver and maker of fine linens, which she sold at high prices to the nobles. She involved, and employed, members of her family as seamstresses, weavers, dye makers, and managers of the Inn.

Rahab Speaks…

I was not a harlot! I was an astute, cunning and shrewd business woman. I had an uncanny ability to negotiate my way out of anything. I was a property owner. I owned this inn built into the wall. My ownership extended from the ground floor to the roof top. That made me a wealthy inn-keeper. I was a single mother, and the sole provider for my children. My husband left years ago - went off to war, and I never heard from anyone about what happened to him. My parents, sisters, and brothers all lived with me and helped with running the inn.

It was a profitable enterprise. My most important commerce, though, was spinning flax on my rooftop, and turning that flax into fine and coarse linens. I targeted my market and my customers. My brothers went to the fields, with my instructions, and bought the flax, using some of the money from the inn's profits. The coarse linen was sold for commercial use -canvases, tent making, military clothing, ship sails and such. The fine linen took careful and delicate hands and was very expensive. My mother, my sisters and I spent many hours sewing this fine linen into clothing for the nobles. The profit it brought was worth it and made for a very wealthy lifestyle. I also negotiated with the dye makers to get beautiful colors for my linens. By law, the bright scarlet and purple could only be worn by the highest nobles. Talk about a monopoly! I spent some days in the marketplace trading, selling, and listening to the news of the day, picking up gossip from the travelers, merchant traders, and soldiers from afar.

Jericho was a prosperous town with a lot of riches and treasures. Many artisans, craftsmen, scholars and merchants lived here. We felt very safe behind the very thick walls of the city. Decades upon decades Jericho was a peaceful, prosperous place to live. Suddenly, we began to hear disturbing news. A horde of strange, savage, barbarian fighters was headed our way, destroying every town, city, and village in sight. Most of the citizenry were not too worried. After all, our walls had protected us against every invasion. But I was uneasy. I began to listen closely to the soldiers and tradesmen coming in. Then we began to get refugees, people running from war. I knew then we were in trouble. Walls or not.

I began to make plans. When I saw two suspicious strangers looking around and watching everything, I knew right away that they were army spies. I made friends with them, and invited them to meet my sisters and talk with my brothers. For three days they ate dinner and had wine with us. The wine loosened their tongues.

That night, we heard the guards coming up the street. We knew they had gotten word of these spies. I started to negotiate with them, for in those three days I had learned everything I needed to know about the invading hoard they represented. I struck a deal and told them I would hide them, lie to the guards, and get them out of the city. In turn, they would agree to keep my family and friends safe. I had no doubt that these strange fighters and their ark would destroy our beloved city. They agreed and I rushed them up the stairs, onto the roof, and under the stacks of flax, with instructions to stay there. If they were found, my life and that of my family's would be forfeit.

We hid all of our expensive goods in cellars with trap doors; the same place we would hide during the fighting. Our brothers and other neighbors left the city by the back gate, with wagons of goods, grains, and bags of our precious coins, to hide in the mountains and caves. Hopefully, after the fighting, we would be able to rebuild our city and our commerce. The scholars, artisans, and merchants began to leave in droves, hoping to make it to the mountains and return after the fighting. I then hurried the spies out by letting them down the back wall using scarlet linen cords.

One week later, we saw the dust rising, an indication the army was closer. My neighbors and I tied scarlet cords on our windows and around our door jambs, a signal that we people were not to be harmed (shades of the Passover). The army approached the city then stopped and sat down at the gates. Suddenly, they stood and began to march around the city. They did this for six days. On the seventh day, they marched and blew their horns. The city walls began to tremble and shake. That strange ark the priests carried emitted a loud humming, buzzing sound that made us grit our teeth. It sounded like a million bees all gathered in one hive. The walls shook and finally collapsed into small boulders and stones. The army came at us like wild animals and uncivilized barbarians. Brave men died fighting and the women and children hid in various underground shelters and tunnels. Everything was completely destroyed, even the beautiful architectural wonders of the crafts and guild halls. The artisan's works were vandalized. The commercial district was ransacked and set afire.

There would be no rebuilding after this! Some of the hide-a-ways were found and the people were killed or assaulted. After a week, things quieted down. The two men who I had hidden found us under the rubble, still in our cellar. I was carried to their leader, Salmon. I asked the reason for the destruction of our city.

He shrugged, "Our God told us to!"

I was stunned!

We were a peaceful, thriving, prosperous place with malice toward none.

He then mumbled something about wanting our treasure and making us worship their God Jehovah.

I could not believe they destroyed our city and our peaceful way of life for that.

He said, since leaving Egypt, they had plundered and fought and murdered their way across the desert for forty years, seeking somewhere called the "The Promised Land."

A question arose in my mind. Why would their God send them on a marauding, killing spree to take land and treasures belonging to others? And were they going to fight all of their days taking other people's land and lives?

I married Salmon, but I was determined that I would not become a camp follower. There was another business opportunity. I convinced him, as leader of the army, the horde, that it was most advantageous for me to set up a small settlement in the ruins of Jericho, and to take the sewing women with me to make suitable clothes for the ragged horde. Contracts were made, and the business began. Other women came to work the flax fields, tended the animals for food, grew the grain, and established community gardens. After a year, the army moved on, but the women remained. Some of the men decided to stay with us for our protection. My brothers returned, bringing our hoarded goods and coins with them. I immediately began to set up a trade route with other cities. Jericho was back on the rise!

After several years of intermittent visits, I decided to settle down with Salmon in what they called the Promised Land. They were still fighting so it did not look that promising to me. Hopefully our son, Boaz, will have a better life than this continuous fighting and serving a warrior God.

What Rahab Knows

Leverage Your Leverage

In exchange for their protection, Jewish spies partnered with Rahab, agreeing to save her and her family from the hands of oppressors. Once she confirmed she had something valuable to offer in exchange, Rahab began to barter. In her wisdom, she saw an opportunity and seized it. She did not flinch or faint. Given the small window of escape, the shrewd businesswoman took notice and moved swiftly.

Regardless of who Rahab was known to be, or what she has been known to do, she recognized leverage. The spies were in need of coverage and Rahab believed she could provide it. She could have easily sent the gentlemen to her neighbor's home or questioned why her estate was chosen as a safe haven. But she did neither. The men wanted to save their lives and Rahab wanted to save the lives of her family members. She traded lives for lives and made history as a result.

Leverage may be referred to as "taking full advantage of." In the case of Rahab, she definitely leveraged her skills and resources. To negotiate in this way, you must first recognize your possessions as valuable in the eyes of others. Likewise, the value you place on your possessions must resonate with worth. What if Rahab believed her quarters were not adequately prepared to devise obscurity in any effort to mask the spies? What if she doubted her ability to face the oppressors with courage while deceiving them? The outcome of her life and the lives of her family members might very well have been much different.

In order to leverage what you have, you must first acknowledge the magnitude and potential impact of what you have to offer. Many times we overlook skills, resources, connections, talents, and experiences because they come naturally, easily, or are familiar. Often what is in front of us is taken for granted and not recognized as valuable. This happens in all facets of life. We neglect to nurture long-standing friendships and relationships or disregard the person in the office who is not as educated as we are, or who hasn't attained the level of success we have experienced. Rahab's experiences cue our awakening, not only to the ways we view others, but also to the scrutiny of ourselves.

Learning to take full advantage of your skills, resources, and connections will open even more doors to success. Where are you short changing yourself? Identify areas where you are downplaying the gifts you bring to the world. The universe graciously compensates competence and awareness.

Assess your skills, relationships, connections, experiences, and talents. Where can you leverage your leverage to influence outcomes?

How can you use your leverage to help someone else?

Hold on to HOPE

The idea that everything will work out for the best is plain optimism. However, as Rahab assured the spies of her plans for their safety, there was more than optimism. She embodied a spirit of hope within her soul. From this perspective, hope was different than optimism. Yes, it's great to maintain a positive outlook and to present an attitude of cheer with an expectation for the best. But hope moves beyond the bounds of passively waiting for all to be well. Hope infers activity, an agitation in the sense of continual movement. Rahab had more than a positive outlook. There was a belief that works, or actions in faith, thrive. This evidence was found in the act of "doing" to affect outcomes rather than "waiting" optimistically, expecting the outcome to be pleasant. Hope motivates a confrontation that brings challenges. There is an acknowledgment of obstacles, but also confidence in knowing obstacles don't matter.

There are many times along life's journey where life will pitch a curveball. They come in the form of health challenges, relationship fall outs, financial downturns, heartaches, and disappointments. But while holding on to hope there is confidence, an unwavering reliance upon force that operates much bigger than you can fathom. In hope, there is heart, spunk, assuredness. Hope combats cynicism and quiets the inner critic. Even if the matter does not yield your desired outcomes, there is security in knowing it will work together for good. Jeremiah 29:11 reads, *"For I know the thoughts that I think toward you,"* says the Lord, *"thoughts of peace and not of evil, to give you a future and a hope."* This declaration of hope is more reliable than stocks, bonds, contracts, or agreements. A partnership, a marriage that is irrevocable, is formed in the depths of hope. Of all life's events and relationships where you can place an expectation, invest in the One with a proven track record.

"Hope breeds possibilities and possibilities breed opportunities"

Stimuknowlogy Institute

Identify a situation or concern in your life where Hope will serve you well. Infuse hope and reevaluate.

"Thus also faith by itself, if it does not have works, is dead" (James 2:17). What actions are you taking, or can take, to exercise the ideals of faith more abundantly?

Preparation Propels the Plan

Anyone would hardly argue against the fact that Rahab took a huge risk in betraying her country. To hide spies meant she was willing to sacrifice her life and the lives of her family members. Sacrifice. An interesting word. Sacrifice often refers to relinquishing something or to give something up at a loss. Except in the account of Rahab, the "giving up" or relinquishing was anything but a loss. By all measures, Rahab gained more than any prized possession or fame could extol upon her. Through acts of preparation, belief, and courage, she was rewarded with a life that served as a testimony to the entire world.

On wings of faith and with hope in her heart, Rahab cleverly planned both the protection and escape of God's messengers. Although there was no evidence to suggest she was aware that this event would take place prior to the men arriving, there were reports suggesting her belief in a higher power. Because Rahab's heart was prepared, she was able to make quick decisions in abetting the spies. Thank goodness for her belief and self-confidence.

I am often asked about confidence and the role it plays in building a business. For me, confidence evolves around preparation. Like Rahab, the more prepared you are, the more confidence you can demonstrate in the process of execution. In part, the act of preparation begins long before an expected end. Many times, the end itself may be vague, or apparently elusive. Nonetheless, an expectant soul is always ready despite the present circumstances.

Moses was another excellent example of propelling the plan through preparation. For forty years he served as a shepherd. It was in the season of preparation that Moses learned valuable lessons about leadership. When charged to lead the Hebrew people from the bondage of the Egyptians, he was equipped to carry out the task with confidence, knowledge, and with the hope for success.

In pursuit of passion, we often neglect the need for preparation. The ground to receive is often founded on purposed preparation.

"There are no secrets to success. It is the result of preparation, hard work, and learning from failure."

Colin Powell
Retired four star general of the United States Army

Think of something you would like to achieve or obtain within the next three to five years. What preparations can you take now to activate the universe towards reception?

How have you or can you, use lessons from failure to prepare for success?

Chapter 8
LYDIA: THE ULTIMATE BUSINESS WOMAN

There is no virtue in being poor! There is no virtue in begging! There is no saving grace in being dowdy, shabby, unkempt, downcast, frumpy, or "acting" meek and humble. One can show one's blessings by approaching life boldly and assertively, using those God-given, innate skills, earned and learned, and employing the senses to make life better and richer.

Lydia was a consummate business woman, rich in mind and graceful in spirit. She was intelligent, shrewd, independent and showed her blessings by being considerate of others. She was kind and compassionate and surrounded herself with like-minded people. Her hospitality was well known throughout the area. Her kindness and philanthropy were also well known. Her Christian beliefs, combined with her business acumen, served her well in many 'sticky' economic and social situations.

Lydia Speaks...

I was very successful and very independent. I built a large enterprise through negotiations, hard work, and an acute awareness of opportunities. When the opportunities come, I was prepared to act on them. I had a lucrative dye works company, a textile company, and a weaving and cloth making company where I produced fine linens and tapestries for the nobles. I employed tent makers and leather workers. When the Silk Road from China opened, I was ready. I had spent some time in the marketplace where news circled and buzzed like flies. Traders, merchants, and ship captains began to talk about the beautiful, exquisite material that had never before been seen - a material that had been woven from a worm and was incredibly expensive. I, being a wealthy woman, was given an audience with the Governor. By the end of the meeting, I had negotiated a very good deal, a license, and a monopoly on this material before it hit the marketplace.

Shades of commerce. My business instinct told me that was going to be extreme. When the beautiful material arrived on our shores, the Governor paid me a visit. He made a decree that only the nobles could wear the beautiful purple stuff called silk. All royal babies would be wrapped in the material at birth. Thus was coined the phrase, "born to the purple." I received orders from other towns and cities for the beautiful purple dyed cloth. I sent textiles, linens, and tapestries, but I did not send the silk. The Emperor himself sent an envoy to purchase all that I had. Talk about "supply and demand"! I was indeed wealthy beyond belief! My purple dyed silk would go down in history. With the monopoly I held, the silk would continue to come to me only.

Even with all of my business and economic gains, I still managed to stay in touch with my spiritual essence and keep my prayer life at the forefront of my mind. We were in a place of prayer, a quiet place down by the river, away from the hustle and bustle of the city, when we were approached by Paul and Silas, two men who had come to the city preaching about a Savior and His kingdom in the sky. They talked about love, mercy, forgiveness, and grace. They were constantly being ran out of cities, or thrown in jail, for preaching blasphemy about a Son of God.

It was strange but comforting. I wanted to know more about this new doctrine. I invited them to come and spend a few days at my estate and to teach me and my household about this new way of thinking. More people came to hear him, and my house became the meeting place for the discussions. I employed scribes to write down the sayings and the words of the speakers. Paul and Silas remained at my house for a month, teaching and preaching daily. By this time I was quite proficient as he was in teaching this enlightened gospel. When they were preparing to leave, I handed them a leather purse filled with coins that they could use to support themselves while traveling and preaching. I instructed them to stay in touch and to let me know where they settled. I told them I'd send more money for the establishment of a more permanent meeting place.

Some of the poorer people of the town began to gather at the gates of my house, and I invited them in to hear the words being spoken. After the teachings, I distributed food and money. I had to limit these meetings to once a week so as not to interrupt my businesses and economic concerns. After all, I had to make money in order to use money.

As this gospel became more popular, my house, my estate, became the first church. My blessings continue.

What Lydia Knows

Goodness and Kindness are Rewarded

Lydia's kindness cannot be discounted. Blessed with talent, riches, and resources, she took care of business and looked after her community. There was no doubt she understood, *"For everyone to whom much is given, from him much will be required;"* (Luke 12:48). She was savvy, stylish, and strutted with authority. When Paul and Silas needed shelter, Lydia graciously provided. And, she didn't stop there. Because she was hospitable and always willing to serve, her home became the meeting place for Christian worshippers. Historically, this was noted as the birthplace of the first church of Philippi. What a legacy!

With grace and humility, Lydia served others. Although considered a well to do woman, she did not marvel in her wealth, nor did she separate herself from the masses. Instead, she was mindful of the needs of others, and treated everyone, both rich and poor, with respect. Her life was an example for all in that, no matter your position, goodness and kindness are always rewarded.

I believe something special happens in the universe when we look beyond ourselves and to the need in someone else. This very act of servanthood was demonstrated by the greatest leader who walked the earth. In Genesis 4:9, Cain sarcastically asked, *"Am I my brother's keeper?"* The reply is simple. "Yes, I am my brother and sister's keeper." Living in this manner adds meaning to our existence and gives purpose to life. We are all called to serve one another in humility and love (Galatians 5:13). Sharing your time or other resources, extending a hand of compassion, or doing something for someone that they simply cannot do for themselves, reflects goodness and kindness. Lydia's life was a model for us to consciously and willingly serve others. It is true, *"The moment you give, you receive at the same time."*

Identify an organization or non-profit you are willing to extend goodness and kindness to over the next six months. What is your plan for serving?

Make a list of five people who you can express goodness, kindness, or compassion towards. Surprise them unexpectedly.

Be Good to You

If you take a close look at Lydia's life, you will find that she had class and style, and that she enjoyed the finer things in life. According to Scriptures, Lydia was a businesswoman who dealt in purple cloth. During Roman times, cloth dyed with purple was a rarity and high in demand. Royalty draped themselves with the delicate fabric, portraying prosperity and elitism. Using her resources and intellect to produce, market, and sell the finest silk, Lydia was able to carve out a life that not only provided a means to survival, but one that also afforded her a life of luxury. She was entrepreneurial, influential, and an ultra-chic woman.

I love the quote by Sir Thomas Browne:

"But how shall we expect charity towards others,
when we are uncharitable to ourselves?
'Charity begins at home,' is the voice of the world."

Further study of Lydia's business sense and style revealed one who undoubtedly took care of herself as much as she tended to the cares of others. In today's lingo, some may describe her as "a show stopper –dressed to the nines." Sparing no opportunity to spoil herself, Lydia did what so many women in today's society neglect to do…cherish themselves. She understood the benefits of beginning charity at home.

As a reminder, you are your most precious resource. How you treat yourself will determine how others respond to you. In loving yourself unconditionally, you also demonstrate the ability to purely love others. Self-care is so important, the Lord commanded it as a foundational Law.

"'You shall love the Lord your God with all your heart, with all your soul and with all your mind.' This is the first and great commandment. And the second is like it: 'You shall love your neighbor as yourself.' On these two commandments hang all the Law and the Prophets."

Matthew 22: 37-40

If Lydia could speak directly to the contemporary women, I can imagine her saying something like this: *"Permission granted to indulge."*

On a scale of 1 to 10 (10 being the highest), how well do you take care of yourself (physically, mentally, spiritually, emotionally)?

Today, create a Personal Self-Care Plan. You are so worth it! See an example in Appendix D.

Prioritize the Important

According to several different resources, Lydia played a significant role in the start-up of the church at Philippi. She was not only a successful business owner, but there were many reasons to believe she was a woman searching for a higher spiritual experience. As was mentioned before, Lydia met others daily on the edge of town near to a river. There, the prayer warriors gathered to affirm their faith, and to wait to meet others who passed along the shores, all the while spreading the gospel. Although an extremely busy solopreneur and breadwinner for her family, she still found time to pursue a deeper connection at the source. Some researchers suggest Lydia was aware that she needed to be covered by mercy and grace. At the marketplace, competition was fierce; a girl needed all the help she could muster. As a result of prioritizing and devoting time to what she deemed most important, truly, goodness and mercy followed her.

Wise women know, amidst all the hustle and bustle, time is needed for discernment. In these moments, perhaps it's time to reflect on and prioritize life's most important matters. To discern is to suggest discovery. When you make an effort to be insightful, new experiences usually ensue. Hence, experiences bring greater lessons and the opportunity to prioritize worth and value. This is the time to consider your personal brand, your legacy. 1Corinthians 2:15 encourages us to *"judge all things."* Laying all cares aside, what do you, (absolutely and unequivocally) want to be known for twenty, thirty, or even forty years from now? Now is the time for careful consideration of your actions, motives, intentions, desires, and values. Focus daily efforts with sustained energy.

"Pursuit of perfection is futile. Instead, I prioritize and often realize goals or tasks I've been aiming for just aren't that important."

Aisha Tyler
American Actress

Take inventory. Where do you need to prioritize - to reflect areas in your life that are most important?

George Washington Carver, American botanist and inventor, compels us to look closely at our works and pay attention to legacy… *"No individual has any right to come into the world and go out of it without leaving behind him distinct and legitimate reasons for having passed through it."*

Complete The Life Ledger activity as found in Appendix E. What are your highest values to pass along to generations to come?

Chapter 9
WOMAN: THE VIRTUOUS ONE

Who can find a virtuous woman? This poem is a song to the goddess, Wisdom. She is mentioned often in Scripture and inferred even more.

It began with King Lemuel re-telling advice given to him by his mother, Bathsheba when he was looking for a suitable wife. In modern day it is interpreted as the worth and wisdom of a woman, a working woman, who brings in a paycheck while the husband apparently does nothing but live off of her earnings. While she works, he sits at the gates (under the trees, at the pool) drinking palm wine (beer), gossiping about his non-existent sex life, playing checkers, or betting on the chariot races with shekels and credit cards she has given him.

She is the ultimate, enterprising, business woman. She is a mover and shaker of enterprises. She is an educated, skillful negotiator, and an expert in the ways of commerce. She can even best the hagglers in the marketplace or the boardroom.

The Virtuous Woman Speaks…

If virtuous means working hard, working long hours, managing my household and my employees, going to the marketplace to hear the local gossip, keeping up with the business trends, keeping my eye on the commerce, and seeing what sells and what doesn't, then, yes! I was virtuous.

I referred to myself as the CEO. I was the BOSS. My household, my estates, my vineyards, my fields, my employees (some family), spinners, weavers, planters, households guards were all paid by me.

When I met with the merchants and ship captains, I was confident I could reach a good and profitable deal by making each side feel like they had won, profited something. Good business!

My parents recognized my acute negotiating skills and sharp intelligence at an early age. They saw that I could predict the market values and read the faces of the merchants. I could tell if they were honest or devious. My mother taught me household skills, but my business and commercial skills came from my father. My wider education came from tutors and visiting scholars who gave me a world view of the way things were. I was taught confidence, independence, assertiveness, and a "stand straight and look people in the eye" type of social upbringing.

My days as a child and as a young adult, consisted of going to the market early with my father to hone my business skills, taking lessons with the teachers in the afternoon, engaging in household duties, and practicing social graces in the evening. I loved every moment.

When talks of marriage began, I brushed them aside. I was not interested, and my family could not force me. I was having too much fun helping my mother run the estate, making business deals, and getting rich with my father. My sisters had married and moved out. My brothers could not understand my obsessions with worldly things instead of the insular life of a pampered wealthy lady of means. Some of my friends made fun of me, and others envied my freedom and growing riches.

Finally, I fell in love with one of the scholars. I evaluated the situation. He considered himself an intellectual (my intellect was higher). What I needed was a spouse who would not interfere with my business acumen or butt into the running of my household.

Aha! This could work!

We would both benefit from this and be happy. We had a big week long wedding and moved into a lovely estate I had recently purchased on the outskirts of town. After a while, we settled into a very comfortable routine.

Each morning, he headed to the gates where he taught or had discussions with the other elders. I sent him nice dinners of lamb rolls, bread, olives, yogurt, baklava, and a handful of shekels to buy palm wine or fermented figs.

Meanwhile, I had deals to make, lands to buy, and ships filled with spices to meet. I bought and traded with the merchants, hired planters for the vineyard, and inspected the spinning and weaving before the linens went to market. I had to deal with tutors and nurses for the children, making sure they were well dressed and attended to lovingly. At least once per week, I took alms and food to the poor and still kept myself looking lovely and well dressed.

Yes! We were praised in the gates, but I did not forget where all of those blessings came from or flowed. I spent time at dawn in introspection and spiritual reflection. I gave thanks every day for a family who saw my worth and value as a young child and proceeded to nurture and shape that child into a young woman full of grace, compassion, and love. A woman wise to the ways of the world. I was a good wife because I chose to be. I had the means to be any way I chose. My skills, my training, my intelligence, my business acumen, and my wealth, allowed me to choose my destiny. Praise God for virtue.

What the Virtuous Woman Knows

Control that Chatter

Okay, I know what you're thinking. This woman is too good to be true. Well, think again. The virtuous woman is all that and more. She is angelic, yet fierce; resourceful, yet reserved; bold, but humble. On all accords, the virtuous woman is an all-in (all hands on deck) type woman. For sure, this is not your average girl. I don't think so. Phenomenal woman. That's "V."

No matter what version of The Book you peruse, pay close attention to the words used to describe the virtuous woman. Words matter. So much so, Proverbs 18:21 warns, *"Death and life are in the power of the tongue."* Neuro Linguistic Programming (NLP) considers the dynamics of the mind -language connection, and the impact on both behavior and the physical body. According to this school of thought, communication patterns affect what you think and the way in which you behave, thereby influencing the physical responses within the body. If this is a valid premise, then disempowering language disempowers, and empowering language empowers. Each type of language shows up in the physical body in different ways. Language, similar to thoughts, generates vibrational energy. In effect, you have the ability to alter your emotions by altering your language. Ponder this thought for a moment and consider the chatter that goes on inside your head. You know, that self-talk that is constantly nagging and seems to be never ending. Words mirror thoughts. Thoughts translate to behavior… action. How do you show up in the world? Honestly? Are your fruits representative of your potential? Notice your language and consider whether it is congruent with your inner talk. Scrutinize the conversation you have with yourself and connect the dots.

Think about your thinking. What are the thoughts that consume much of your airtime? Is it encouraging or discouraging?

How are the thoughts you harbor, showing up in your physical body? Are you fatigued, energized, anxious, healthy, unhealthy, depressed, mentally well and grounded? What are the physical indicators that all is well, or that there is work to be done?

Redefine Mediocrity

Proverbs 31:10 asks, *"Who can find a virtuous wife?"* The verse goes on to say, *"For her worth is far above rubies."* Of the entire verse, these two lines alone paint a picture of a woman who is rare, accomplished, and to be honored. It would seem that she has all she needs and could ever desire. Yet, the passage continues to pour out accolades and traits to be admired. Certainly, extraordinary has been catapulted beyond comprehension. The virtuous woman stretches the band of what is possible when there is constant and consistent evidence of progress.

One of the greatest dangers to success and achievement is the accomplishment therein. I often refer to this as 'arson by arrival.' This is the effect of becoming so accomplished that one becomes consumed by the thought of having arrived or succeeded, that you are at the destination. Dead end. Get off the bus. Right? However, when you analyze the definition of mediocrity you see the terminology often applied to things, people, and places that are "commonplace, everyday, run-of-the-mill." In other words, mediocrity refers to that which has become the norm or routine in marginalizing or flat lining at the present level. In essence, whatever heights you have achieved up to this point, if you are no longer growing, you are stagnant, dabbling with mediocre tendencies.

For a few, this may be a tough notion to digest. But in all fairness, if you are not *intentionally* growing, learning, developing, and setting new targets, then you risk becoming mediocre at best. Notice the word "intentional" is emphasized to draw attention to that which is deliberate and planned. Intentional growth is not the training or professional development a supervisor or company suggests or offers to expand company goals. Instead, this is a conscious plan of action initiated by you, for you, through you.

Who are your personal (intentional) development mentors? How do they help you stretch beyond your current level of mediocrity?

Outline your intentional personal development plan. Consider books to read, places to visit, people to share time with, classes to enroll, and quiet time in reflection.

Fun Fuels "Fantabulism"

So, I am well aware you will not find "fantabulism" in the dictionary. But, for the sake of creativity, let me take a moment to explain this coined terminology. As you have probably guessed, the words *fantastic* and *fabulous* were combined to frame fantabulous. The addition of "ism" implies a "system, practice of or an artistic movement." In this case, "fantabulism" is a movement to create something that is awe-inspiring. Although the expression is not used in the description of the virtuous woman, I imagine that was the way she likely emoted and lived her life. Proverbs 31:29 declares, *"Many daughters have done well, But you excel them all."* This sounds like a woman who enjoyed who she was and who she became. There was a sense of "can-do" attitude in a spirit of flare. The virtuous woman's swagger is exhilarating, far reaching, and life altering. Ultimately, she was the evidence that *"how you do life, determines how life does you."*

As the virtuous woman went about life, in all she did, an element of contentment, stillness if you will, appeared to abound. This was not someone who performed work with an attitude of resentment. No, this was the makings of a joyful heart; one who soared to the limits of faith and fun. Fun is the root of enjoyment, as she delighted at the work of her hands.

At this juncture, I yield to contemplate the spirit in which I do the work I do, and my temperament within different relationships. Perhaps you might linger too for a moment and consider the woman within. Is she having fun? Does she find amusement in her day? Is there a quest for zest and jubilance? These and other thoughts may come to mind. In general, the sentiment expressed in any area of your life spills over to reveal itself in all segments. If the end is the goal, enjoy the process. Start a revolution - a movement of FUN!

"I am going to keep having fun every day I have left, because there is no other way of life. You just have to decide whether you are a Tigger or an Eeyore."

- Randy Pausch
American Professor

What are you doing to foster a fun, fantastic, and fabulous life?

Identify the patterns, habits that have become boring and seemingly laborious. How can you shake up, or add spice to the routine?

Chapter 10
WOMEN OF TODAY: TAKE ACTION

It is my sincerest hope that you have laughed, sighed, and even gasped while recounting history from the perspective of biblical women as only they can tell. Each shared a view that was quite different from mainstream accounts. As alluded to at the start of this journey, multiple perspectives often challenge our deep rooted beliefs and interpretations of what is right and wrong. In general, judgment takes a strong hold of thought as we struggle to understand ideas, beliefs, and values outside our defined norms. Here, it is important to recall the source of perception. Your judgment is based on your sole experiences. However, as a behaviorist will tell you, the map is certainly not the territory. This means your views are based on your experiences and are unique to you. Each of us is equipped with a slightly different map, which ultimately leads to slightly different ways of thinking about any given topic. To change your current map or perceptions, you must be exposed to different experiences, or maps. Hopefully, *REvision* has extended a platform for you to do just that.

We generally see things as we wish them to be, rather than how they really appear. As you create a plan to live even more deliberately and intentionally powerful, you will develop a keen sense of purpose when perception is expanded. This is most often attained through quiet speculation and an honest assessment of where you are psychologically, and a discovery of how you got there. For this reason, opportunities for reflection were included at the conclusion of each story to guide a deeper introspection through practical applications. The questions were designed so that you could contemplate effectiveness in your everyday life as either a mother, daughter, aunt, sister, in-law, or as a career focused - business minded woman. Avenues to better understand and align purposes are generally discovered through active participation. Purpose guided by passion provides opportunities for new insight and fresh beginnings.

Still, the real wealth is in your thinking. Therein lies a natural resource to design and create almost anything you can imagine. Vision, a resource that is often untapped or used sparingly, can be life altering and far reaching, so much so that legacies and lineages are created through its lens. *REvision* invites you to rediscover and fulfill your potential in ways that captivate your heart. Just as you have encountered different perspectives in the lives of women from the Bible, you are encouraged to take a second look at the reservoirs of your soul. Maybe, just maybe, the female spirit is more powerful than anyone has ever suggested you consider. Dig deeper, allow revelations from 2000-year-old principles to influence your contemporary lifestyles.

APPENDIX A

Personal Mission Statement

Mission is determined by who you were created to be. A mission statement is usually stated in generic terms and sets a statement of purpose for what you wish to accomplish. Most personal mission statements are abstract and reflective in nature. It clarifies purpose and an explanation for your existence. In writing your Personal Mission Statement, ask yourself several guiding questions.

- What are my innate gifts, skills, and experiences I can share with the world, leaving it better than I found it?
- What are my three to five deepest values? Why are these values important to me?
- How can I live mentally, physically, socially, spiritually whole?
- How can I complete all of the roles I play in life (family, professional, local community, globally)?
- What can I do to share my gifts with the world and contribute to a better world?

Example:

"My mission in life is not to merely survive, but to thrive; and to do so with some passion, some compassion, some humor, and some style."

- Maya Angelou
Poet, Civil Rights Activist

APPENDIX B
PERSONAL VISION STATEMENT

Vision is about the future. It is the ability to look beyond the present and behave in ways that influence what is to come. It activates the imagination more than immediate circumstances. Through visioning, you are able to prioritize what is most important and to see beyond yourself. Vision isn't simply about you. It connects to humanity, service, and the essence of the greater good. Vision recruits clarity and inspires the soul. Consider several questions when you create a Personal Vision Statement.

- What does Spirit (God, Universe, Source) want for my life?
- What do I want my legacy to be?
- What unresolved global issue nags at me continually?
- When I think of my future, what do I see?
- When I think three family generations forward, what do I envision?
- What is most important to me?
- What are my audacious dreams, goals, desires, hopes?

Example:

"To use my gifts of intelligence, charisma, and creativity to impact millions around the world in experiencing the power of awareness and meaningful in significant ways."

- Dr. Larthenia Howard
Author, Entrepreneur

APPENDIX C
DEFINITION OF SELF (PURPOSE) STATEMENT

A Definition of Self-answers the basic question of "*Who Am I?*" Basic. Not at all. This goes beyond "what you do" and the different roles you play in various areas of your life. Who you are may be more about your philosophical "nature." That is, what do you identify with that persist over time? Who you are defines the essence of your existence.

example:

"I am a gifted and creative spirit purposed by the Creator to communicate through divine insight, the offering of peace, hope, and possibilities."

- *Dr. E.*
Author, Entrepreneur

APPENDIX D
PERSONAL SELF-CARE PLAN

A Personal Self-Care Plan outlines your self-care initiatives in areas connected to your overall wellbeing. The purpose of this plan is to optimize your life, so you are available to give to yourself and others. You are encouraged to develop a plan inclusive of activities, events, people, and places that bring you joy, peace, and happiness. It is suggested that you review your plan for self-care regularly to ensure that you follow through and make updates.

Key Area	Activity	Possible Barriers	How to Overcome Barriers
Emotional	• Deep Tissue Massage • Oil diffuser and sound wave app	• Cost • Time for massages	• Include in monthly budget • Membership options • Schedule in calendar
Physical	• Walk inside/outside • Low carb/high protein diet • Use stairs when possible	• Travel schedule is hectic	• Use hotel gym • Exercise in hotel room, follow fitness YouTube channels
Spiritual	• 15 minutes meditation/study in a.m. • Bible Study • Interest group meetings	• Consistency • Travel schedule	• Set morning alarm • View online services • Join Egroups
Relationships	• Confront issues as they arise • Call daughter once weekly • Lunch w/co-workers once weekly	• Fear of confrontation • Few healthy eating venues near office location	• Journal thoughts and possible outcomes for issues • Pack lunch for office meetings
Finances	• Saving deposit w/each paystub • Include recreation & tithing in budget • Increase 401K investments • Investment club	• Overspending • Unexpected spending	• Separate accounts for different purposes • Automatic withdrawals in 401K

Key Area	Activity	Possible Barriers	How to Overcome Barriers
Emotional			
Physical			
Spiritual			
Relationships			
Finances			

APPENDIX E
THE LIFE LEDGER ©2017

The Life Ledger is designed to help you recall meaningful accounts of your life and the impact those events have had in shaping who you are and who you are becoming. Part of the process is to identify influencers (those who have helped to cultivate your beliefs, values, character), places, things and events from which you have drawn life lessons. This is intended to be a journey you can share as a legacy with a special person or group of people. What do you want them to know about you? What are the highlights of your life, lessons learned that are valuable? Why do you want to share the selected events? How can your legacy offer insight, wisdom, guidance?

(Note: This activity is used with permission from the Stimuknowlogy Institute LLC and is part of Building a Legacy Lantern module.)

Fiscal Year (Year of the memory)	Chart of the Account (Event as remembered). Include as many details as possible – location, sites, sounds, people, smells, etc.	Deductibles (Meaning, message, value that you gained)
1993	The day our son was born, my life completely changed. What a joyful experience. The medical staff rushed in…….	Life is fragile. Breath is precious. Treat them respect by living on purpose, with intention, daily.
2000	The day he asked for a divorce for the 2nd time within a three year period. We were driving along the turnpike returning from a family gathering. Our son was in the back sit asleep, six years old at the time. I was completely…..	Love yourself enough to be able to recognize when others don't, no matter how badly you wish them to.

THE LIFE LEDGER ©2017

Fiscal Year (Year of the memory)	Chart of the Account (Event as remembered). Include as many details as possible – location, sites, sounds, people, smells, etc.	Deductibles (Meaning, message, value that you gained)

"No one, when he has lit a lamp, puts it in a secret place or under a basket, but on a lampstand, that those who come in may see the light."

- Luke 11:33

REFERENCES

Women in the Bible

Eve: The Truth Teller…Genesis 2 and 3

Jezebel: The Queen…1 Kings and 2 Kings

Mary: The Magdalene… Matthew 27:56, 61; 28:1; Mark 15:40, 47; 16:1-19; Luke 8:2; 24:10; John 19:25; 20:1-18

Priestess of Endor: The Sibyl…1 Samuel 28

Deborah: The General…Judges 4 and Judges 5

Thecla: The Preacher…Acts of Paul and Thecla – Apocryphal New Testament

Rahab: The Business Woman Renown…Joshua 2: 1-24

Lydia: The Ultimate Business Woman…Acts 16: 12-15

Woman: The Virtuous One…Proverbs 31: 10-31

Quotations

This book contains quotations from the following public figures and organizations: Maya Angelou, Sir Thomas Browne, Warren Buffett, George Washington Carver, Thomas Edison, Albert Einstein, T. Harv Eker, Randy Pausch, Colin Powell, George Bernard Shaw, Aisha Taylor, Quintus Septimius Florens Tertullianus, and Zig Ziglar; Mediawebapps and The Stimuknowlogy Institute.

Scriptures

Genesis 1:7, Genesis 1: 27-28, Genesis 3, Genesis 4:9, Judges 5:6, Judges 5:24, Proverbs 3:5-6, Proverbs 18:21, Proverbs 31:10, Proverbs 31:29, Jeremiah 17, Jeremiah 17: 8, Jeremiah 29:11, Jeremiah 44:17, Matthew 6:23-24, Matthew 22: 37-38, Luke 11:33, Luke 12:48, John 20:17, John 20:11-18, Romans 8:11, 1 Corinthians 2:15, Galatians 5:13, Ephesians 6, Colossians 3:23, 2 Timothy 4:7, James 2:17, Revelations 2:8

Books

Maxwell, J. C. (2007). *The Maxwell Leadership Bible: Lessons in Leadership from the Word of God* (2nd ed.). Nashville, TN: Thomas Nelson Publishers.

Pagels, E. (1989). *Gnostic Gospels.* New York, NY: Vintage Books.

Online Links

Defining Who Am I?

https://www.youtube.com/watch?v=UHwVyplU3Pg

http://ed.ted.com/lessons/who-am-i-a-philosophical-inquiry-amy-adkins

Mission Statement Generator

www.msb.franklincovey.com

Philosophy- History: Locke on Personal Identity, Part 1

https://www.youtube.com/watch?v=462Y898PVn8

CONNECT WITH REVEREND SPRADLEY TO SUCCESSORIZE YOUR NEXT EVENT

Mistress of Ceremony

Keynote Speaker

Workshops Facilitator

Moderator

Guest Panelist

Lecturer

spraddunn@yahoo.com

THE REVEREND CLAUDIA W. SPRADLEY

Author * Spiritual Leader * Social Worker * Therapist * Hospice Chaplain

Ideas that challenge the status quo as they inspire are indeed the most powerful. Often, these ideas are met with resistance because they shift paradigms, shaking institutions to their core. In religious spaces, revolutionary thinking is often viewed as irreverence. The Reverend Claudia W. Spradley has been a wielder of such ideas since becoming ordained in 1985.

Known as "The Irreverent Reverend" to her congregation, she was never satisfied with viewing women of the Bible solely through the male lens. After decades of study, a generation of practice as a theologian, and years of well-traveled research, Rev. Spradley has authored *REvision*, a vital new work for the canon of writings on women in the Bible.

Born and raised among nine siblings in West Palm Beach, Florida, Rev. Spradley credits her mother, grandmother, and other strong women in her life with encouraging education and high moral standards. Her academic career has been lifelong, with Rev. Spradley earning her Bachelor of Science degree in English Education from Florida Atlantic University, her master's in Social Work from Barry University, Ordination from the AME Ministerial School, and her Master's of Divinity from Directed Independent Studies. Rev. Spradley also studied at South Florida Theological Center, and Evangelical Bible College and Seminary.

During her Seminary studies, Rev. Spradley found kindred academic spirits in professors of Greek Testament and Women's Studies, who affirmed her desire to expand the ways in which women of scripture were written. She knew early on that their dynamism deserved more exploration. "I did a paper on the concept of the Trinity. In it, I questioned the absence of the woman and the appearance of the nebulous "Holy Spirit" in her place. Then I began to question all of the negative views of the woman. I began to do research. After realizing that the scriptures were simply a collection of stories, I became a storyteller. What better way to reach the everyday woman without using the boring, stuffy theological terminology?"

REvision sets about the work of revealing women of scripture in their full and most dynamic glory, as women of great intelligence, skill, and virtues beyond chastity and fidelity. Rev. Spradley earned the name The Irreverent Reverend with what she describes as a penchant for "seeing the humor, wit, conflicts, controversies and some absurd ideas in the scriptures," and speaking on them. "To preach on the woman's role in religion will cause anger, hostility and in some cases derision," she observes. "Most are comfortable in their boxes, and do not wish to step outside, or to give women an equal place. My favorite woman in the scriptures is The

Magdalene because of her strength, her fortitude, her ability to withstand prejudice, sexism, and persecution and still speak her mind. Many scholars believe that The Magdalene, along with Priscilla, Huldah and Thecla wrote much of the scriptures."

Rev. Spradley understands that this ministry is not the chosen path for so many theologians because of the threat of backlash, but for Rev. Spradley, the connections between women of scripture and today's modern women are undeniable. "Women of that time were about the business of surviving, leading, taking care, managing, preaching, teaching and running their businesses, shops and homes." These connections are the foundation of *REvision*, and seek to amplify the voices of women of scripture in ways that affirm women of faith and avid readers everywhere. After many years of research and travel to the places where women of the Bible lived, including Italy, Greece, Israel, and parts of Africa and Asia,

Rev. Spradley tells the *her*story of women in scripture like no other author to date. "I tell the stories through the eyes of the women themselves, as parables. Their spirits were most insistent that I tell their stories, and now I have." More to come…